Have We Had This Conversation?

Have We Had This Conversation?

Lasting Words for Establishing Choral Excellence

by John Yarrington

SCHOTT BRADSHAW
PUBLISHERS LLC

6700 WOODLANDS PARKWAY, STE 230-288
THE WOODLANDS, TEXAS 77382

Several publishers have kindly granted us permission to include excerpts of various copyright works. Please see pages x–xi for a complete list of these compositions and their publishers. For the complete copyright notice, please see the first page of each excerpt.

Editors: Sally Schott and Janice Bradshaw
Book Design: Digital Dynamite, Inc.
Cover Design: Patti Jeffers

Schott Bradshaw Publishers LLC
6700 Woodlands Parkway, Ste 230-288
The Woodlands, Texas 77382

Exclusive Distributor

The Lorenz Corporation
P.O. Box 802
Dayton, OH 45401-0802
www.lorenz.com

Printed in the United States of America

ISBN: 978-1-4291-0338-1

For Diane Strohmeyer,
wonderful colleague,
treasured friend.

Conversation. Association or social intercourse; intimate acquaintance. Familiar acquaintance from using or studying. Behavior or manner of living (archaic).

Conversational quality. A manner of utterance that sounds like spontaneous, direct communication.

Contents

List of Music Examples - x

Guide to Score Markings - xii

Foreword - xv

Acknowledgments - xvii

Introduction - 1

Chapter One: The Conversation Begins with Text - - - - - - - - - - - - - - - - - - - 6
An exploration of how the text guides all of our work—from the initial presentation to all elements of interpretation. After all, the music is in the words.

Chapter Two: The Conversation Continues with Careful Score Study - - - - 24
Goals and approaches to gain an understanding of both the parts and the whole, all with the goal of enlightening our singers.

**Chapter Three: Without Appropriate Gesture,
the Conversation Is Impaired - 48**
Techniques to quiet the body and improve the effectiveness of each gesture.

Chapter Four: Preparing the Ensemble for the Conversation - - - - - - - - - 68
Build and nurture the voices—and persons—in your choir with purposeful and targeted warm-ups.

Chapter Five: Rehearsal Is the Lifeblood of the Conversation - - - - - - - - - - 74
Strategies and suggestions for planning and structuring your rehearsal to get the most out of each meeting.

Chapter Six: What Do They Need for the Conversation? - - - - - - - - - - - - 79
From the practical to the inner-personal, this is what will truly elevate your teaching.

Chapter Seven: What Do I Need for the Conversation? - - - - - - - - - - - - - 84
An important reminder not to neglect our own needs, and tips for fulfilling them.

Chapter Eight: When In Our Music - 87
An in-depth conversation about the role of music and singing in the church, and how we can further that role.

**Appendix: Biographical Information of Selected
Choral Composers and Conductors - 96**

Notes - 100

Music Examples

Chapter One

Thee We Adore (CM 492)
Setting by T. Frederick H. Candlyn
Published by Carl Fischer, Inc., 65 Bleecker Street, New York, NY 10012
Phone: (212) 777-0900 • Fax: (212) 477-6996 • cf-info@carlfischer.com • www.carlfischer.com

Concertato on Holy God, We Praise Thy Name! (G 3167)
Setting by John Ferguson
Published by GIA Publications, Inc., 7404 S. Mason Avenue, Chicago, IL 60638
Phone: (800) 442-1358 • www.giamusic.com

O Magnum Mysterium (HMC-960)
Thomás Luis de Victoria, edited by Walter S. Collins
Published by Hinshaw Music, Inc., P.O. Box 470, Chapel Hill, NC 27514
Phone: (919) 933-1691 • Fax: (919) 967-3399 • www.hinshawmusic.com

Chapter Two

Sanctus in d minor (BWV 239) (AMP 0361)
J. S. Bach, edited by William Hunt
Published by Alliance Music Publications, Inc., P.O. Box 131977, Houston, TX 77219-1977
Phone: (713) 868-9980 • Fax: (713) 802-2988 • info@alliancemusic.com • www.alliancemusic.com

Great and Glorious (64065)
Franz Joseph Haydn, arranged by Charles F. Manney
Published by Belwin Mills Publishing Corp.
Distributed by Alfred Publishing Co., P.O. Box 10003, Van Nuys, CA 91410-0003
Phone: (818) 892-2452 • Fax: (818) 830-6252 • customerservice@alfred.com • www.alfred.com

There Is Sweet Music Here (15/2143H)
Mary Lynn Lightfoot
Published by Heritage Music Press, A Lorenz Company, P.O. Box 802, Dayton, OH 45401-0802
Phone: (937) 228-6118 • Fax: (937) 223-2042 • info@lorenz.com • www.lorenz.com

Chapter Three

First Light (DH0406)

Daniel E. Gawthrop

Published by Dunstan House, P.O. Box 7, Jonesborough, TN 37659

Phone: (423) 610-0028 • office@dunstanhouse.com • www.DunstanHouse.com

I Will Sing and Give Praise (HMC-299)

Alice Parker

Published by Hinshaw Music, Inc., P.O. Box 470, Chapel Hill, NC 27514

Phone: (919) 933-1691 • Fax: (919) 967-3399 • www.hinshawmusic.com

Chapter Eight

When In Our Music God Is Glorified

Text by Fred Pratt Green

Music by Charles Villiers Stanford

Copyright © 1972 by Hope Publishing Company, 380 South Main Place, Carol Stream, IL 60188

Phone: (630) 665-3200 • Fax: (630) 665-2552

hope@hopepublishing.com • www.hopepublishing.com

Guide to Score Markings

Full-length bar lines indicate sections of the piece.

Slurs are marked to indicate phrasing.

A check ✓ indicates a breath.

A **comma** ⟩ indicates a lift.

Parentheses indicate an unaccented syllable.

A **large dot** above or below a note, •, indicates that it should be light and un-accented, or is an upbeat. It is not a *staccato*, so does *not* indicate that it should be short.

A horizontal **brace** ⌐‾‾‾¬ indicates a grouping, e.g. 2+3 or 3+2.

A **down arrow,** ↓, identifies a destination point.

A **horizontal arrow,** ⟶, indicates a line's direction and destination.

A **curved arrow,** ↰, indicates that the consonant should be sung ahead of the beat and the vowel should be sung on the beat.

The **schwa** is marked with ə.

FL indicates the syllable should be sung with one flip of the R.

For example: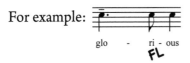

A **vertical line through an R** indicates that it should not be sung.

For example: Ld

DIH indicates that the final "D" should be sounded as "dih" not "duh."

A **circled syllable**, such as in "myri-um," indicates a destination; the line should move toward this syllable.

An **underlined syllable** shows emphasis or weight.

Consonants are added to a score to heighten awareness of the importance of consonant articulation in all styles, including legato.

In the example below, the **slash** indicates that the dot should not be sung.

Similarly, when a tie functions as a dot, as in the example below, a **line or slash** indicates that the tied note should not be sung.

In the example below, the **slash** indicates a lift to facilitate articulation of the sixteenth notes.

Foreword

This book is so readable you won't realize how much you're learning until you begin to apply the information to teaching or concert preparation. Each page provides a wealth of practical and helpful information applicable to school groups, church choirs and community choruses.

This publishing project has provided us with the opportunity to bring the wit and wisdom of John Yarrington to a broad audience. It represents our beliefs that:

- The marriage of text and music is an essential element of creating meaningful presentations of choral works.
- Effective rehearsals lead to quality performances.
- A systematic approach to rehearsal preparation is the foundation for successful teaching.
- Musicality is taught every day, in every way.
- An honest analysis of how conducting gestures affect singers can lead to improved communication.
- Music-making involves understanding those who are making the music.

Have We Had This Conversation? is for conductors who want to provide the highest quality experience for their singers. Just as humor is a key ingredient in this book, so should it be an important aspect of your rehearsals. It is our hope that reading this book will cause you to learn and to laugh!

Janice Bradshaw
Sally Schott
Schott Bradshaw Publishers LLC

Acknowledgements

Wonderful teachers: Alice Parker, Bev Henson, Ann Howard Jones, Anton Armstrong, John Ferguson, Jim Jordan

Treasured colleagues: Kevin Riehle, Ken Axelson, Sid Davis, Craig Jessop, Joby Bell, Robert Linder, John Ricketts, Len Bobo, Jim Maase, Rhonda Furr, Richard Fiese, Melissa Givens, Jane Gawthrop

Composer friends: Dan Gawthrop, Morten Lauridsen, Dan Forrest, Mack Wilberg, Ann Gebuhr, Dan Kramlich

HBU student conductors: Chris Jones, Dusten Melear, Matt Parker, Ruben Alcala, Dominique Royem

Publishers: Larry F. Pugh, The Lorenz Corporation; Janice Bradshaw, Schott Bradshaw Publishers

Excellent, exceptional grandchildren: Peyton, Carson, Hayes, John Robert

Finally, to Diane, wife and companion, for many years of steadfast love and for grace and forgiveness freely given. I don't deserve, but gratefully receive. Love you!

A huge thanks to Sally Schott, my friend of many years. Without your hard work, this book would never have seen the light of day.

Introduction

Picture the following scene: The choir is rehearsing *Great and Glorious* by Haydn, an anthem they know well and perform frequently.* I find myself reiterating the following:

- *Remember:* The "gr" of "great" goes before the beat as does the "gl" of "glorious." Also, the "r" in "glorious" is flipped.
- *Remember:* Don't accent unaccented syllables, even after the bar line. Example: "MA-jes-tee" not "ma-jes-TEE."
- *Remember:* The bar before the middle section slows to prepare this section. There is no marking in the music, and none is needed. The cadence clearly shows that musically one section is ending while another is beginning.

  Also, at the bottom of page 9, finish the phrase "truly, upon him." Breathe and phrase before the pick-up, "the Lord upholdeth."

I then heard myself remark out loud: "Have we had this conversation?" It reminded me of a saying by my teacher, the late Bev Henson: "If you are tired of hearing me say this, think how tired I am of saying it."

I confess that the phrase "Have we had this conversation" is usually spoken with considerable emotion and is definitely rhetorical. I *have* spoken about these issues as we've rehearsed anthem after anthem. We have marked them; we have practiced them; we have joked, cajoled, stomped, made faces. Yet, the same type of unmusical interpretation happens again and again.

Hence the title of this book, representing both the frustration and the promise of working with school, church or community ensembles. We want our choirs to sing with appropriate style, phrasing, musicality, diction, and articulation. And, we work at it constantly. Often, it seems, we go over and over the same ground, don't we?

Let me begin our conversation with some observations on...

---

*   See pages 37–42 for musical excerpts from this piece.

…Text

- Alice Parker, American composer, speaks about notation as the "black blobs." She maintains that the blobs tell only about five percent of what is needed to attain significant musicality. In other words, printed symbols can convey only so much meaning, particularly when they are associated with text.

  When we teach notes, we must also teach the grouping and articulation of those notes as well as the musicality of words, the direction of phrases and the dynamic range of each section of the piece. To "put the music in" after notes are learned is to ask for, at best, correctness devoid of expression and, at worst, unmusical singing.

- Speaking text can introduce the choir to its beauty and meaning. A thoughtful reading with careful attention to inflection reveals word shapes and phrase destinations. It should always be done mid-voice, sensitively and not in any kind of sing-song manner.

- Making a radical commitment to the vowel (an Ann Howard Jones phrase) means never singing anything except the most beautiful, well-shaped vowel possible. The idea that we learn correct rhythms and pitches and then put beauty in is, of course, nonsense.

…Rehearsal Strategies

- A choir's initial encounter with a work should allow for as much musicality as possible. Deciding where to start, and with what, is crucial. Often, playing the piece straight through is a good first step. A recording is also valuable, as it can provide an overview and generate enthusiasm and excitement about the piece. I believe that the initial introduction to a new piece, whether it is an anthem or a larger work, is among the most important presentations one makes.

- It is crucial to build the ensemble at every meeting. This means warming up and tuning up. From the first sounds in the rehearsal room, all must work for beauty of sound and accurate pitch. Doing anything less does not build the ensemble to prepare it for the music to come.

- Continuity of rehearsal attendance is key, whether in church or school. For instance, many church choirs suggest that their members should not sing if they have been absent from rehearsal. College or community choir attendance should be no less stringent. Those who have been faithful in rehearsal do not deserve the "drop in" attitude of a few divas. Moreover, the music cannot be made at the appropriate level under these conditions, because a cohesive ensemble is the essence of music-making. Ensemble means being together in both rehearsal and performance. One cannot be separated from the other.

- The more *a cappella* work we do, the stronger our group becomes. When there is too much dependency on the piano, it can become a crutch. Rather than reinforcing the parts with the keyboard, let singers flounder a bit. Encourage them to rely on their eyes and ears to negotiate their own vocal line. Use numbers or solfége as an aid to reading. Place a good deal of the responsibility on the singers to figure out the visual and aural cues they need to accurately sing their parts. Above all, be encouraging as each singer builds his or her music-reading and listening skills.

- Sectional rehearsals, especially in church, are helpful. Those leading the sectional rehearsals should have a grasp of the overall concept of the piece so that the expressive aspects of the music are always foremost, regardless of correct or incorrect notes.

- We work to develop listening skills. Starting with the warm-up, maintain high expectations for discriminating listening and concentration on establishing and maintaining good intonation. A warm-up without attention to tuning is a prelude for disaster. Every singer needs to be engaged, and every singer needs to understand that a high level of concentration is absolutely essential to a productive rehearsal.

- Appropriate gestures incorporated into rehearsal segments serve as an aid to developing musicality. Asking the singers for a simple arm-sweep to indicate phrase shape or instructing them to point for individual pitches are simple but effective approaches. Asking the singers to conduct using a standard conducting pattern gets them physically involved. Encouraging physical response to various aspects of the music builds a cohesive ensemble in addition to expanding the singers' expressive capabilities.

- Rhythmic movement is important. Establish the basic pulse by clapping or tapping. In music that is particularly rhythmic, such as early American hymns and spirituals, a left-foot downbeat with purpose establishes a sense of pulse and provides appropriate rhythmic sense and direction. Often, we confuse speed with excitement. Establishing a basic pulse allows for that excitement but also helps keep the choir from running away with the music. It is not necessarily true that the choir that rushes together stays together.

- Seating the choir in a formation where parts are mixed (what John Ferguson calls "singing confused") can be effective, but only if each singer knows the music very, very well. To be surrounded by other parts is a listening challenge and quickly reveals the insecurities of individual singers.

...Repertoire Selection

- In a school setting, it is important to explore a wide variety of styles and ranges of difficulty. This is no less true in a church setting. In both instances, often "I know what I like" really means "I like what I know." For example, I don't find college students all that ready to turn away from their affection for nineteenth-century music to attempt Des Prez or Palestrina on the one hand, or Stravinsky or Britten on the other. If one's stylistic comfort zone is late Classical or early to late Romantic, Palestrina is far removed, as is Stravinsky. Church singers often voice the "seven last words" (we've never done this that way before) when pushed outside their comfort boundaries.

- What continues to surprise and please me both at the university and at church is how quality music wins support so easily. As conductors, our study of essential musical and stylistic elements gives us direction as we introduce and teach unfamiliar works. Interesting recordings and insightful writing bring performance practice into perspective. If one wants to perform Bach motets, there are numerous recordings of the same works, each displaying choices quite different in terms of performing forces, tempi, articulation, and the like. No conductor gains understanding by simply copying someone else's performance. Rather, one's skill is honed by listening to and comparing performances. It is a great time to be alive and making music, especially choral music, for the opportunity to study varied interpretations of classic works is readily available through a wealth of recordings.

- We must have challenges. Obviously, exposure to a variety of styles and degrees of difficulty puts our groups on the path to developing ever-increasing skills and musical understanding.

Questions remain, such as:

- Why do we tend to sing Bach or Haydn in the same way that we sing Schubert or Brahms?

- Does "pounding pitches" really accomplish a musical result?

- How can we encourage our singers to be receptive to different tonal approaches, articulation, phrasing, etc., to get a more stylistically appropriate interpretation?

- Should we take responsibility for building the ensemble so its capabilities embrace the music chosen to rehearse and perform?

- What are effective approaches that will equip our singers to be more aware of the differences in performance practice in various stylistic periods?

These questions, as well as the preceding observations, will be explored in the coming chapters. In Chapter One, we will focus on text. Subsequently we will deal with score study, conducting gesture, ensemble building, and rehearsal strategies. The pieces listed below will be used to open up our conversation. For each, we will explore its history, ways to find its sound, and performance possibilities and teaching strategies (which includes performance practices and potential notational difficulties) as they relate to the topic of the chapter. Extended excerpts also follow each presentation to help further the conversation. (Those of you who have read Alice Parker's *Creative Hymn Singing* will recognize our categories of history, finding the sound, and performance possibilities, as they are subtitles in this text.[1])

Music Examples
- *Thee We Adore*, setting by T. Frederick H. Candlyn
- *Concertato on Holy God, We Praise Thy Name!*, arranged by John Ferguson
- *O Magnum Mysterium*, by Thomás Luis de Victoria, edited by Walter S. Collins
- *Sanctus*, Johann Sebastian Bach, edited by William Hunt
- *Great and Glorious*, by Franz Joseph Haydn, arranged by Charles F. Manney
- *There Is Sweet Music Here*, by Mary Lynn Lightfoot
- *First Light*, by Daniel E. Gawthrop
- *I Will Sing and Give Praise*, by Alice Parker

As we examine each of these selections, be sure to ask:

- What kind of piece are you?
- Do you have brothers and sisters?
- Are there other pieces written by this same composer?
- What do you know about the total output of said composer?
- Are there recordings to aid understanding?
- Do you remember *anything* you learned in music literature or music history?
- Can you apply what you learned? (Ah! There is *the* question!)

Chapter One
The Conversation Begins with Text

"The music is in the words" is a phrase composer Daniel E. Gawthrop uses to describe how he looks at a text before setting it to music. The musical notes (or "black blobs" as Alice Parker refers to them) don't just attach themselves to words in random fashion. Rather, the music is a direct product of the composer's sensitivity to the beauty, nuance, shading and weight of various syllables in the text. Speaking text aloud, pausing to listen, weighing important syllables, and listening for where the words want to take us is the simplest way to begin. This will lead to an immediate sense of the direction and development of the phrases within the piece. To learn the notes first and then add the words is backwards.

If the text is not substantive, poetic, interesting and/or engaging, I am simply not interested in looking further. If the text is familiar (from a mass or a scripture passage), I am intrigued to see if the music enhances, underscores and makes real the music in the words. If it doesn't, I am not interested. I desire a text to which I may return with expectation. It must have beauty and meaning, offer a challenge, and demand artistry. A worthy text to put before my singers is always uppermost in my mind when selecting music.

I believe that the initial contact with a new piece should start with text in careful, loving, interested, attentive speaking. If the music *is* in the words, this is readily apparent. If the text is trite or repetitious, the music has no chance to make it better. "He ain't heavy, he's my brother" may work as a popular song, but the most skillfully constructed music cannot redeem faulty, ill-chosen poetry.

Words are important; one might say crucial. How much do words weigh? How much are words worth? (Wordsworth! Is there a Longfellow here?) Rehearsing is teaching, and teaching begins with text. To what purpose are all those correct notes, beautiful sounds and well-tuned chords memorized and sung by bright-eyed choristers in lovely robes or tuxedos? If the substance of words, their meaning, their grouping together toward destinations is not achieved, what is the point? Might this be a form of "clanging cymbals?"

I see, as do you, gentle reader, many anthems where the text has been forced into the music without regard to the relative importance of the word or the natural stress of the syllable. All too many pieces feature trite phrases that are repeated with equally trite, uninteresting music. Life is short; why bother?

Those of you who have read my other books know how much in debt I am to American composer Alice Parker. She continues to champion the importance of text and to believe that one *begins* with text. I am the second generation of those who espouse her ideas. Her manifold compositional output; her incisive writing about text and music; her unique ability in this country and abroad to draw from common, ordinary folk the most beautiful, artistic sounds in hymn sings—all speak to her love of the incredible singing endeavor. In her work with Robert Shaw, text has been foremost in consideration. (The name Robert Shaw has been synonymous with choral music for several decades. For more information about his role in the development of choral music in America, please refer to the Appendix.)

In the book *Dear People,* there is a wonderful anecdote about Parker's first experience with Mr. Shaw. Parker was admitted to Juilliard in the fall of 1947 and auditioned for the Collegiate Chorale, but didn't measure up. Said Mr. Shaw: "If you want to be a choral conductor you've got to learn to sing better than that." According to Parker, "he let me in anyway, on the condition that I always sit in the back row and never let him hear me."[1]

A hard-working student, Parker observed every rehearsal of the Collegiate Chorale, the "small choir," and the Juilliard Chorus, taking meticulous notes of everything that went on, right down to the number of minutes Mr. Shaw devoted to each step in a rehearsal.

Impressed by her musicality and industry, Mr. Shaw asked her to try writing an arrangement for him. As she remembered, she "brought him what must have been the world's worst arrangement. In one place, there was a florid sixteenth-note contrapuntal line with no words to it." He said, "What do they sing there?" I replied, "Oh, you put that in later." And he said, "Oh, no you don't." "I was thoroughly insulted, but it didn't take me long to catch on that you've got to begin with words."

The process of composing with the text foremost is called *wordsmithing.* Says Parker:

We don't often think about this in relationship to the texts of our choral works. We take for granted that they've always been there, created whole, without the intervention of choice of other possibilities, and move quickly on to study the notes. Poems evolve just as music does, with innumerable choices and often hard-wrought decisions.

If someone wants to score-read my composition, the act of studying the notes without a prior understanding of the poem can only lead to a misunderstanding of the whole.

I can only assume that my experience is similar to song composers before me. A sensitive word-setting never occurs by accident. Settings by Bach and Schubert and Brahms and Gershwin always betray an intuitive knowledge of the way the text flows off the human tongue, as well as "what it means." I have a theory that lyric poets have a truly musical understanding of the rhythms and colors on which speech rides.[2]

For several years, Parker has led a small group of conductors and musicians in two or three days of score reading, an event in which I recently participated. As Parker describes, the intent of the work done at this event is "to look at compositions of different periods, discover what they communicate and how they are constructed. This is not at all from a theoretical or musicological perspective, but rather from a humanist, common-sense point of view: What was the composer's relationship with this work, and how can I, the reader, make it mine?"

Thee We Adore

Setting by T. Frederick H. Candlyn
SATB and Organ
Published by Carl Fischer, Inc.

History

Based on Gregorian chant where the rhythm of the music *is* the rhythm of the words. This is worship music, music that does not call attention to itself. Chant was a practical way to intone scripture.

Finding the Sound

Begin with careful, expressive reading (intoning) of the text, listening for the natural rise and fall of important syllables, and pausing (lingering) over those. Take, for example, the first vocal line (m. 9–12):

> THEE we a-DORE, O HID-den SAV-iour, THEE,

Intone the text on a single pitch (mid-range), allowing important syllables (which are capitalized above) to have that lingering quality. Nothing here is metrical. Ask this of your choir members: "sing with absolute humility, as though you are singing to yourself." Encourage them to let that humble approach be reflected both in their musical concepts and their vocal expression.

Performance Possibilities/Teaching Strategies

Candlyn has added barlines in his edition that would not have been in the original chant notation. Further, I have added some articulation markings to the excerpts found on the following three pages. The musical goal of these additions has to do with achieving an intoned quality with the natural rise and fall of the text determining the flow of the music. Remember, this is worship music that is devotional in nature.

As directors, our voice is our best model. We demonstrate with utmost nuance, color and style, and we listen to the choir's response. As we continue to nurture the sound and its word-rhythm (not metrical rhythm) we understand that:

- Bar lines are only organizational.
- The "black blobs" represent pitches, *not rhythms*.

- This is not music with which to demonstrate one's superior vocal technique. The singing is subservient to the text, functioning very much like an accompaniment to the words.

- Throughout, this Gregorian melody is prominent, especially in the four-part setting that begins in measure 50. Those not possessing the melody must give it access and be sure they are hearing melody as they sing their own parts.

Thee We Adore

Anthem for Mixed Voices (S.A.T.B.)
Founded on the Plainsong Hymn "Adoro te devote"

Translated from
St. Thomas Aquinas

T. FREDERICK H. CANDLYN

*The small notes may be taken by a few Sopranos.

Concertato on Holy God, We Praise Thy Name!

Setting by John Ferguson
SATB, Congregation, Organ and Optional Brass Quartet
Published by GIA Publications, Inc.

History

This anthem is based on an ancient Te Deum melody combined with the hymn GROSSER GOTT, from the *Katholisches Gesangbuch*, written in Vienna, circa 1774.

The setting of the Latin Te Deum text is Gregorian chant, or plainchant, where the function of the music is to convey or intone scripture. When the hymn is combined with the chant, it moves in a triplet rhythm with a sense of one beat to a measure.

Finding the Sound

Allow the singers to discover the natural flow of the words by speaking the text expressively, with careful attention to the role of important words and stressed syllables (which are capitalized below) as destination points. For example:

> Te DE-um, lau-DA-mus:
> te DO-mi-num con-fi-TE-mur.

Intone the text on a single pitch (mid-range) with a nonmetrical approach, which provides the flexibility necessary to give appropriate emphasis to important syllables. Each singer should strive for a sound sung more to oneself than as a demonstration of vocal prowess.

The hymn tune text should be approached in the same way, speaking the text as a poetic whole, listening for the rise and fall of important syllables and/or words:

> HO-ly GOD, we PRAISE your NAME
> LORD of all we BOW be-FORE YOU.

Performance Possibilities/Teaching Strategies

The score markings in the excerpts that follow include additional articulation markings as well as circles around various syllables. These syllables should be weighted but not accented. One sings toward the next circled syllable. The musical goal is to capture the intoning quality of the text in an unhurried fashion.

When the hymn tune enters, the quarter note establishes a more metrical framework without sacrificing the Te Deum chant.

By modeling the desired approach to tone and text treatment, one develops the choir's sense of intoning the text and utilizing the kind of tonal quality that serves as a vehicle for the music.

The coda comes full circle with a final statement of the chant combined with a final statement of the hymn text: "Through the Church the song goes on."

Concertato on

HOLY GOD, WE PRAISE THY NAME!

For SATB voices, congregation, organ and optional brass quartet

Grosser Gott, wir loben dich
Ascr. to Ignaz Franz, 1719–1790
Tr. by Clarence Walworth, 1820–1900

GROSSER GOTT
Katholisches Gesangbuch, Vienna c. 1774
Setting by John Ferguson

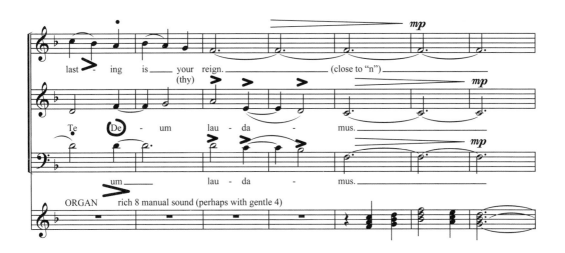

···················· *Coda* ····················

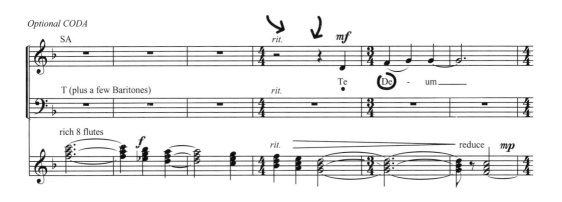

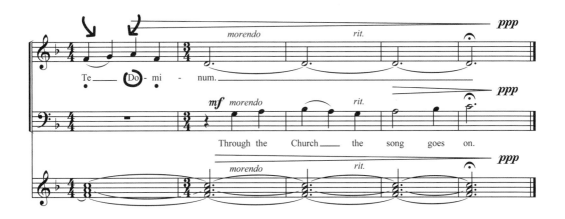

O Magnum Mysterium

Thomás Luis de Victoria, ed. Walter S. Collins
SATB and Optional Keyboard
Published by Hinshaw Music, Inc.

History

For this piece, we have an authoritative edition by Walter S. Collins. It is one in a series of editions of public-domain choral masterworks, many of which have been published many times before.

The general editorial policies on display in this series are:

1. To provide vocal scores in modern notation containing everything the composer left, including original performing forces and original language.
2. To add nothing to what the composer left without it being clearly identified as editorial. The piece, its source, the editorial method, the text, and performance practices are presented skillfully and fully.

Finding the Sound

This work is best performed by a small ensemble using a quality of tone that has the clarity and lightness to balance with the sound of boy sopranos. Use moderate dynamic and tempi changes and support the voice with sustained organ. Collins directs us to sing the lines "with very careful attention to phrasing and to the natural accents of the words."

I am always amazed that singers tend to sing with "their" sound, regardless of what is appropriate to the piece. I hear Renaissance music sung with rich sounds that are full of vibrato as if it were Brahms. I also hear this music sung with thin, uninteresting, colorless tone as well. As conductor/teacher, one models the sound in all of its nuance and color so that individual ears will tune up to the infinite possibilities of appropriate sound. Have one section at a time sing their lines as others listen. When another line is added, the conversation begins; that is the essence of the sound and performance practice of this style. The natural energy needed to ascend *and* descend should always be present, but in moderation.

Performance Possibilities/Teaching Strategies

Beginning with a careful, expressive, attentive intoning of text (sound familiar?) we find the essence of a multivoice motet, each line based on Gregorian chant. One of the simplest methods of arriving at accurate performance is to ask everyone to circle the important (weighted) syllables and move the musical line toward and then away from them. Choirs love to accent the unimportant, but we help them hear the difference when the text is treated appropriately.

I love this type of music because each line (each vocal part) is so essential to the whole. When singers understand the importance of the text and its relationship to their individual line, it is a revelation. When their line is joined with the others in the conversation, a most wonderful musical event happens.

O Magnum Mysterium
for Mixed Voices, S.A.T.B., with Keyboard (Optional)

THOMÁS LUIS de VICTORIA (1549–1611)
Edited by Walter S. Collins

a. No accidental in source, which should signify return to flat. *Opera Omnia* has ♮ with ficta flat above.

b. ♮ with note in *Opera Omnia*.

a. In the source the cantus and altus have "me-ruerunt"; tenor and bassus have "me-rue-runt."

a. In the source the cantus and altus have "me-ruerunt"; tenor and bassus have "me-rue-runt."

❝❞

The conversation begins with text.

Chapter Two
The Conversation Continues with Careful Score Study

Careful, systematic score study is the prelude to creative teaching and artistic performance. There is no other way, and there are no shortcuts. I love this part of the process, bringing everything I have learned in theory, form and analysis, and music history and music literature to this adventure, this quest, for answers. Sometimes, I think we, as teachers, do not make clear these connections to living, breathing music. How can one possibly think of beginning the rehearsal process without first assessing all of the performance possibilities of a particular piece? It is essential to examine every aspect. We must look at each detail, using all the knowledge we've gained about individual musical ingredients to gain understanding of both the parts and the whole. Only then are we prepared to enlighten our singers.

As just discussed in Chapter One, the first look at a piece always begins with text. After that, the order becomes:

1. **The work as a whole**—structure, key relationships, textual relationships, accompaniment, melodic construction, and choral or orchestral demands. I try to teach my students to graph a work in the model of Dr. Julius Herford's meticulous work.[1] Dr. Herford used to say that one should be able to conduct from one's graph. Structure and form are wonderful teachers. Understanding harmonic implications, harmonic rhythm and key centers enables one to get into the mind of the composer/creator.

2. **The details.** Mr. Shaw used to remark, "the beauty is in the details." Anyone who has sung with him using one of his marked choral scores knows the relevance of this statement. In my own study, I carefully mark breathing places, specific articulation regarding length of note, accent, and crescendo/decrescendo, and then ask singers to mark as well. Unless it is marked, they will not remember! At Houston Baptist University (HBU) our slogan is: "Marking is a sign of intelligence."

My friend and colleague Jan Harrington used to shout: "I want to see flashes of yellow in front of my face!" The flashes to which he was referring were those from No. 2 yellow pencils. My students know that should I come 'round and pick up an individual piece of music that is not marked, all hell will break loose, and I do not mean theologically.

After study, rehearsal becomes a starting place for an inspired performance. Expecting singers to mark and be faithful to those markings is tantamount to an excellent and inspiring effort. "I feel it such and such a way" is certainly the way—the way to a disastrous performance.

I also believe in trusting singers, enabling them to bring all of their own brain power and artistry to the product. (Read *The Musician's Soul* by Dr. James Jordan.[2]) I believe in encouraging individual musicianship. I call on their care and their sense of responsibility for learning not just the notes but also learning where those notes go and desire to go. I want them to know how many notes should be grouped together. I want them to take responsibility for articulation, dynamics, contrasts of various kinds, and for shaping words and phrases.

When we trust in this way, we also love in the highest sense. The chorus does not actually vote on the repertoire we've selected, but singers display attitudes which quickly reveal whether a piece is to be embraced or rejected. We must act on the belief that they possess enough collective intelligence to carry out the task of rehearsing and performing the pieces we have chosen with a high degree of quality. And, we must show the confidence we have in them by establishing a high level of trust between teacher/conductor and singer.

Caring for individual singers, encouraging them and listening to them is a part of the whole idea of developing an ensemble. Discipline must exist, and often an individual must be corrected, but never in public. Always remain sensitive to each person's feelings. A conductor tirade seldom brings desired results, and one should remember that temperament is 95 percent temper. I will speak privately to a particular singer whose attitude, attendance, lack of attention, or failure to mark his/her score is holding back the entire group. That is my responsibility.

At HBU, we do what we call "weed eating." On a scheduled day, everyone stands up, individually, and sings his/her part of selected excerpts from the current repertoire. The intent is not to embarrass but rather to make everyone accountable. The practice rooms are usually full the days before the weed eating. A grade is given that figures into the final. The intent is unmistakable: You are responsible to everyone else in the choir and ultimately, to the composer.

None of the above is possible, however, without that initial score study by the conductor. Julius Herford speaks about this, using the term *search*.

In an article in the December 1991 issue of *The Choral Journal*, Herford offers these thoughts about score study:

> Skill in learning about a piece amounts to learning from the work itself, not from any interpretation—even the most masterful. No theorist, no authority of style, not even the composer is our teacher; ultimately, only the work itself teaches us. Therefore, we have to learn the language of the work. There is no substitute for it and no way out of it.
>
> The great master composers—Bach, Handel, Haydn, Mozart, Beethoven, Stravinsky and the rest, are in reality composers of the present because the now-living generations need their music. We need to base our lives on the values out of which their music grew. Our goal should be to learn to speak great music so that it becomes our own language.[3]

Bach's *Sanctus*, Haydn's *Great and Glorious* and Lightfoot's *There is Sweet Music Here* are the illustrative pieces for the conversation about score study. A checklist of questions and preparatory steps is suggested at the outset:

1. Look through the score and take in the whole.
2. What music do you know of this composer?
3. Who is singing? Who is playing?
4. What do you know about the text?
5. Is this an excerpt from a larger work?
6. What are the key relationships? Does this piece stay in one key, or is there modulation? If there is change in key, look for the key centers.
7. Number the measures.
8. Speak the text, listening for the natural rise and fall of the words. Important words or stressed syllables generally have more weight (not more accent). Circle the weighted words or syllables as you would in Renaissance music.
9. Look for breathing spots, singing each part out loud.

10. Look for the organization of the piece, as well as its structure. Where are the sections? Where does something end and something else begin? Are there elisions?

11. As you sing each vocal part, make a small check where you, yourself, stumble. You have just identified the likely trouble spots for the choir.

12. Decide on the tempo and the most appropriate conducting pattern.

13. Formulate a teaching strategy: How will you introduce the piece and with what?

14. Make a simple graph.

A word about notation. Alice Parker defines notation as an "aide to remembered sound." We should be aware that much cannot be shown by "the ink." (Orchestral players always ask: "Do you want us to play the ink?") I suggest reading *Up Front!* edited by Guy Webb, especially the chapter "Score Selection, Study and Interpretation," by Gordon Paine, which is excerpted below.

> The thousand-year history of musical notation is the story of composers' attempts to communicate musical ideas on paper. It is also the history of performers' attempts to transform that notation into sound. The art and craft of the performer is known as *interpretation*.
>
> Notation in the Middle Ages and most of the Renaissance conveyed nothing more than pitch and rhythm. Late nineteenth-century composers filled their scores with instructions, not just on tempo and dynamics, but on articulation, phrasing, mood, and tone color as well. Some contemporary composers have prescribed so much specific direction that the result has been to offer little opportunity for the performers to make interpretative decisions.[4]

So where does this leave us, gentle reader? We should not teach and conduct with the "I feel it this way" mentality. Instead, we have the excitement and sheer drudgery of score study to allow analysis and historical knowledge to inform musical intuition. Untrained intuition runs the danger of being capricious and is often a substitute for careful, thoughtful investigation. The key to musical interpretation is a systematic attempt to discover how the composer constructed the music and what "makes it work."

Sanctus in d minor (BWV 239)

J. S. Bach, edited by William Hunt
SATB, Two violins, Viola, and Continuo
Published by Alliance Music Publications, Inc.

History

This is one of five independent settings of the Sanctus, all from Leipzig. There is a *Sanctus in C Major* (BMV 237), a *Sanctus in D Major* (BWF 238), *Sanctus in d minor* (BMV 239) and a *Sanctus in G Major* (BMV 240). Authorities accept that the fifth independent *Sanctus* (BMV 241), also in D Major, is an arrangement from a piece by J.C. Kerli.

Finding the Sound

A student will ask, "Do you want this sung without vibrato?" Answer: I will never ask you to sing without any vibrato, but music in this style calls for a cleaner, lighter sound—a more instrumental sound. While it may be easier to tune without vibrato, I believe that a judicious use of what is the most normal sound for the voice works best. Voice teachers who teach students to open up voices are less than enthusiastic about a non-vibrato choral approach, which can actually impede production.

Performance Possibilities (Conductor Study)

Sections are delineated by text repetition or new text, often with one or more measures of instrumental interlude as a cadential elision (m. 1–7). The cadential elision occurs several times and is a strong structural component.

Text has direction toward the most important word or syllable (m. 16–22) with a tempo allowing the shortest notes to sound.

Observing the slurs, as in measures 28–34, by putting less weight on the second note of each allows a graceful, elegant expression of the text.

Speaking aloud this familiar text, one is aware of weighted syllables:

> SAN-ctus DO-mi-nus DE-us SA-ba-oth

I circle the weighted syllables in each part. I speak each part individually, listening for this rise and fall, always aware not to accent the unaccented. For example, "Deus" should be sung as "DEH-us," not "DEH-US."

In my study, I sing each individual line with appropriate accentuation. I mark the breathing.

I place a small checkmark at sectional junctures or, in many cases in this piece, a slur indicating an elision.

This piece will move in a three pattern at a tempo that allows the smallest notes to be heard musically and sung easily: In this case, the smallest notes are the sixteenth notes on the "mi-nus" of "Dominus" found first in m. 5. The tempo cannot be faster than the shortest note can be accommodated. When I sing each part I am aware of the need for this accommodation.

Teaching Strategies

Everyone speaks the text aloud, listening for rise and fall, and heading for destination places, which are given in all caps in the following example:

SAN-ctus DO-mi-nus DE-us

Again, circle weighted syllables and indicate with a downward arrow the important destination syllables or words.

Chant text on a single unison pitch, careful to observe the weighted syllables and head for destination words or syllables.

Play through the entire piece or use a recording.

Two parts at a time sing, while the other two lightly intone text.

Most of the piece is homophonic. The melismatic passages, however, should be shaped toward the center of the melisma. For example:

SAH-ah-ah-ah-ah-ah-AHN-ctus

The point in all of this is that unless we begin carefully with text and text shape, unless we understand the structure of the piece (sections, key centers, homophonic or melismatic occurrences) and unless each vocal part is carefully nurtured musically, we may have correct pitches but no music.

What I continue to find in conducting classes at HBU and in workshops around the country is that a useful rehearsal plan can only be the result of careful score study. There can be no conversation musically without this effort. For me, conducting *is* teaching in the best sense. I want singers to invest themselves in the music. I want their best intelligence. I want their intuition, conductor-guided. I want an ensemble whose completion is a wonderful musical experience. Whether it is this simple *Sanctus* by Bach or an extended work, the process is the same.

Sanctus in d minor

BWV 239

Four voices, two violins, viola, and continuo

J. S. Bach (1685–1750)
edited by William Hunt

Measures 16–22

Measures 28–34

Great and Glorious

Franz Joseph Haydn, arranged by Charles F. Manney
SATB and Organ
Published by Belwin Mills Publishing Corp.

History

The Gloria is an adaptation from the *St. Cecilia Mass* by Haydn, sometimes known as the *Sanctae Caeciliae in C*, written about 1773. "It is by far the longest mass Haydn wrote and also the most Italian in style. The Kyrie and Gloria alone take 45 minutes. This is a 'Cantata Mass' for concert rather than liturgical use."[5]

Finding the Sound

As mentioned earlier, to arrive at the appropriate sound we should ask the right questions about the piece. The tendency is to sing most pieces *mf* (plus) with a rather full sound. In church, we often refer to pieces like the Haydn as a "holler anthem." This oversung production with little thought for articulation or word shaping can be a rewarding visceral experience but certainly is not stylistically appropriate. From the beginning, we must ask for a cleaner, lighter, more energetic sound and resist adopting the "barn burner" mentality.

We are fortunate to have many good recordings of music from this period, often with orchestral accompaniment, and those might be played as a sound ideal. If one chooses to introduce the piece at the piano, a light, rhythmic approach enforces the desired sound. If "pounding pitches" was a good idea, all of our choirs would sound better. People simply don't listen to that which is pounded. We must find other ways to reinforce the sound concept.

Performance Possibilities (Conductor Study)

Make a graph, delineating sections. One would expect shorter phrasal statements in this Classical work. However, the first phrase is six measures plus a downbeat elision rather than the usual four.

Identify key centers and sections.

Look for duets, as in measures 8–9 and 10–11.

Be aware that the strongest statement is always homophonic, as in the beginning.

Acknowledge the importance of setting up the middle section, which begins at m. 72, with the movement from tonic to dominant (familiar Classical tonality). Preparation begins in m. 71 with a slight *ritard.* anticipating the key-center change and change in dynamics.

Teaching Strategies

Begin with an instrumental approach by singing on a neutral syllable. I suggest "pahm" for longer notes, "doot" for shorter notes, and "doo-bee-doo" for melismatic passages.

Develop the ability to listen and discern where the most important part or parts occur. When all parts are sung at the same dynamic level with little or no articulation the result is a thick, muddy texture that is not true to the style.

General rule of thumb: Don't sing the dots—back away, lighten up. In addition:

- Put the consonant combinations "gr" and "pr" ahead of the vowel.
- Sing with direction of phrase and word shape. For example, move toward the capitalized syllables in the following phrase:

    might-y and lov-ing FA-ther, praise Him for His GREAT-ness,

- Take care that there is a good "oo" vowel in the word "unto."
- Flip the "r" in "glorious," or use the syllable "dee," never an American "r."
- Don't accent unaccented syllables falling on the downbeat. Those include the syllables in parentheses in the following words:

    ma-jes-(ty)

    e-ter-(nal)

    fa-(ther)

    great-(ness)

Continue the instrumental approach with clean entrances and appropriate balance between parts.

Speak text rhythmically and artfully. With this approach, often choir members can hear they are not together and then do what is needed to gain more precision.

Whisper the text. Consonants get lost unless they are emphasized.

Approach high-note entrances with adequate breath and the psychology of "coming down from the top."*

I may work a piece on a neutral syllable for several rehearsals before adding text. When text is added, if the piece is weighed down by vocalization and lack of articulation, I immediately go back to the "instrumental" version. Often, two parts sing text while the other two sing on a neutral syllable.

---

*   In Chapter Four, a methodology is explained for warming up and tuning up. It is based on the idea that we should encourage singers to begin in mid-range and to exercise their mid- to upper-range first in a rehearsal. Beginning a rehearsal with any exercise in the key of C means that we immediately engage the lower register or heavy mechanism sound. This is most singers' strongest register for that is where they speak. When working with children, the first priority is to get them into a "singing channel," which means helping them find their upper registers. Specific examples of vocal warm-ups are found on pages 70–73.

Great and Glorious

Anthem for Mixed Voices

FRANZ JOSEPH HAYDN
Arranged by Charles F. Manney

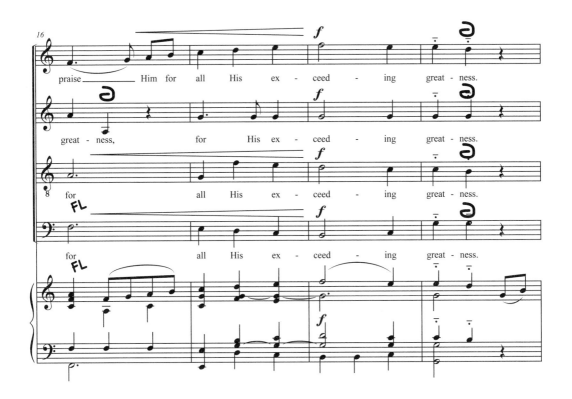

···························· *Measures 37–43* ····························

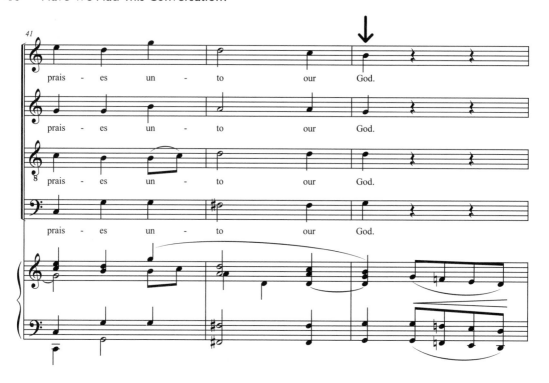

praises unto our God.

praises unto our God.

praises unto our God.

praises unto our God.

Measures 68–88

There is Sweet Music Here

Mary Lynn Lightfoot
SATB and Piano
Published by Heritage Music Press, a Lorenz company

History

This is a well-known text by Tennyson. The music to which it is set is in a romantic idiom with graceful vocal lines for all voices.

Finding the Sound

Begin with careful reading (intoning) of the text, taking care that weighted syllables are observed and, equally important, unweighted or unaccented syllables are not given weight. For example, it is the capitalized syllable in the following words that should be accented:

MU-sic   SOFT-er   PE-tals   RO-ses

Because the music is actually in the words, this care taken with text means that when the music is added, the words flow and weight is appropriate to word shape.

Think about the image of "that softer falls than petals from blown roses on the grass." Or, the idea of "cool mosses deep," "through it ivies creep," and "long-leaved flowers weep."

I fear we have lost our sense of understanding and appreciation for a text such as this. When we "learn" correct pitches and rhythms apart from the words, we are often correct but not sensitive. Hence, the importance of speaking text out loud, listening for the rise and fall of words as well as learning where the destination places (phrases) are.

Obviously, Lightfoot's musical ideas grow out of the text: They are flowing with that wonderful skip of a seventh ("from blown roses"). Never is an unaccented syllable placed on a long note. Always the anacrusic nature of the text ("There is sweet music here, that softer falls,") makes the text sing.

Performance Practices/Teaching Strategies

After speaking text artfully, lingering on important syllables and giving thought to the wonderful pictures painted by the words, begin singing at m. 5 on the neutral syllable "loo" with attention to the natural rise and fall of the melodic contour. Observe my articulation markings in the excerpts on the following pages, particularly those in measures 5–13. Remember that the mark of a dot over certain syllables or words equals light, not short, and that the two-note slurs always mean that the second note of the slur has less weight. Take care that nothing becomes "notey." This happens when all syllables are weighted equally and when no destinations are in mind. Always sing toward the next destination.

In the SATB sections, foster the sense that every part is melodic. A valuable rehearsal procedure is to have each accompanying part sing with the melody, listening for the natural curve and shape rather than plodding along. The same care with word shapes and phrase direction must occur in the bass, alto or tenor lines, else all work in shaping the primary melodic line is for naught.

In the B section (m. 26–29) a different, "cool" tone is set with the contoured thirds in soprano and alto. There is a sense of difference in mood here.

When the A section returns at m. 35, there should be a sense of a heart-warming homecoming—a lifting, delicious sensation of reliving the wonderful moments sung earlier.

There is Sweet Music Here

SATB Chorus and Piano

Alfred, Lord Tennyson (1809–1892), alt
from *Choric Song* from *The Lotos-Eaters*

Mary Lynn Lightfoot

······································ *Measures 5–13* ································

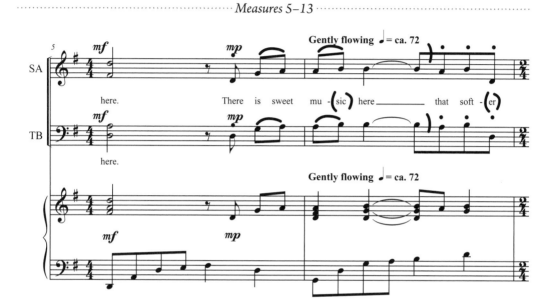

······ Measures 26–29 ······

There are many ways to rehearse, but the clearer the idea about the style and the sound, the better the result.

Chapter Three
Without Appropriate Gesture, the Conversation Is Impaired

I begin the conducting sequence at HBU with the following:

Conductors, You Will Be
Your body is tall, a frame you'll be, so that your gestures all can see.
Not to the right or left do sway
Nor tap your foot along the way.
Your breath "evokes" the singer's sound.
When you breathe well, we all have found
That you can start most any piece...
Start LOUD, start soft, and then release.
With shoulders down, the breath "falls in,"
The breath is "prep," for it's a sin NOT TO BREATHE,
With gesture matching, beautiful sound you'll soon be hatching.
Your palm is flat, your fingers curved in welcoming gesture,
Don't lose your nerve, 'cause "they" will sing—
Upon them call with graceful gestures and body tall.
Now you must trust, RECEIVE THE SOUND,
It comes to you, the sound abounds.
But you can't MAKE or FORCE their singing:
Nor sweat, nor strain sets voices ringing.
When you lean out, with elbows reaching,
You're in their way and thus your teaching
Does not reflect, in gestures clear
Why you and "they" are really here.
Poems are made by fools like me
In hopes that conductors you will be.

Someone might say: "I've seen Robert Shaw rehearse and not only did he sweat, but he changed shirts at the break." Shaw was so intense that he was on fire with the music. I have seen drops of perspiration fall on the music during rehearsal or performance, as have many of you. My use of "sweat" in the poem above does not refer to Mr. Shaw's intense involvement in rehearsing. Rather, it has to do with the prevalence among conductors to overconduct with effortful gesture that never brings the desired result.

Where did we get the idea that we can grunt, sway, clap, snap, run around, sing with them, *and* get beautiful results? Are there conductors that do all of these things and more? Yes. Do they get results? Also yes. However, I strongly believe that there is too much sweating, swaying, and stomping and not enough centering and listening.

We stand still at HBU and learn to receive the sound. Sound is a palpable commodity that can be nurtured and guided by the conductor with clear, concise gesture. Only practice makes this possible. When one uses more gesture than necessary, for whatever reason, listening ability is decreased. When we sing with them, we can't hear them. The more clapping, snapping, stomping and running around we do, the less we stay put and really listen to what is going on.

To this end, I use *Evoking Sound* by James Jordan with accompanying video because I believe it is the best available conducting text.[1] His philosophical approach is based on proper alignment and gesture, always connected with sound. We had the good fortune of having Dr. Jordan as artist-in-residence for a week, and he teaches and preaches what he writes. Imagine!

In the syllabus for the conducting classes I teach, students read:

1. This is a skill-level endeavor, like playing or singing. If you practice, you will improve.
2. You will develop your writing ability, because writing clarifies thinking. Writing is an art and a craft of great importance. An outline of one's thoughts is always a first step to logical, well-written grammatical work.
3. You will keep a rehearsal journal of the ensemble in which you participate, documenting your observations of the weekly process from rehearsal to performance.

    Pause for student question: "When are you going to teach us how to warm up?"
    Answer: "Every rehearsal."

    Student question: "When are you going to teach us how to rehearse?"
    Answer: "Every rehearsal."

4. Score study will be an integral part of your study. Developing the most beautiful and expressive gestures will not result in a musical product. Without the why and what of the musical substance, your technique is useless.

5. We will do much singing in class. Dr. Jordan believes that every gesture should be accompanied by sound. Not all of you will choose conducting as your primary emphasis or life's work, but all of you will benefit enormously from living with, singing, and conducting various styles of music.

What I cannot do in this chapter is replicate what happens in daily sessions. For progress, there must be feedback from the instructor, the class and from individual videos. As one student remarked recently, "Dr. Y., you keep telling me the same things." My response: I *know* other things to tell you but first you need to attend to these.

What I can do in this chapter is encourage you, gentle reader, to assess the effectiveness of your gesture and then do something about it. Another gem from Dr. Ann Howard Jones: "You are through with your rehearsal—you are sweating like a farm animal and your people ask: 'what was that all about?' "

You might be amazed at how much better your group responds and how much better you are able to listen if you clean up your gestures, straighten your alignment, pull across your body instead of reaching out, and quit stomping, clapping, grunting and singing with them.

When I inherit singers at church or school from the overdone school of choral conducting, I have to train them to respond to what I call the grammar of conducting. When I do not cheerlead, they must take their share of responsibility for the music-making. I always conduct with high energy and intensity of purpose but have learned how to shepherd that enormous energy into meaningful gesture.

Perhaps the best way to learn this is to stand in front of an instrumental ensemble. If you are a "choral" conductor, you are already suspect. When you sway, move and talk too much, you confirm their suspicions. When they look up for a downbeat and get something they cannot read, they look down again and begin to count because they know nothing good is coming from the podium. (I speak the truth; ask an instrumentalist.)

With these general ideas, I offer the Yarrington philosophy based on conducting experience and teaching of the craft.

The Yarrington Philosophy

Conducting Credo

I believe in a standard grammar of conducting:

- How and when to start (qualities of beginning)
- How and when to stop (qualities of ending)
- How loud, how soft (range of dynamics)
- How fast, how slow (range of tempi)
- Degrees and varieties of articulation
- Beauty, direction of phrasing (beginning, peak, ending)

I believe that singers and instrumentalists should be trained to respond to standard gesture, universally known and understood.

I believe that singers and instrumentalists must be encouraged to become part of the musical product to make "ensemble" a real word.

Outline of Expectations

1. Learn to economize—less is more; conducting efficiency is the goal.
2. Learn to receive the sound—not reaching, bending, swaying but learning to make contact with the sound you hear.
3. Separate hands for maximum efficiency.
4. Use stance (alignment) to your advantage.
5. Enable "them"; learn not to cross the line between conductor and singer/player.
6. Experience the power of elongation. (A word of explanation: Any beat in a standard conducting gesture can be expanded or elongated to show duration or phrasing destination. When we make all beats the same in our gesture, it is the same as singing all notes the same.)
7. Look like the music sounds.
8. Develop fluency with a baton.
9. Learn to balance perspiration with inspiration.
10. Practice "dry conducting" patterns.
11. Have the score in your head and your head out of the score.

12. Develop precision and poise—the sense of someone in charge.

13. Work on musicality!

14. Work on musicality!!

15. Work on musicality!!!

Making the Right Choice

Much about gesture depends on the music to be performed and the forces involved. A larger chorus with orchestral accompaniment requires a broader gesture, but also one that is clear and precise. A downbeat prepared with the full quality of the opening sound can be life-changing. It may seem simplistic to observe, but when we want something louder, we broaden the gesture. Softer requires less gesture but never a weak one. When you hunch over to indicate a soft dynamic, you exhibit the type of body posture (alignment) that is a negative sign for the singer.

Any beat can show change in articulation, dynamics and tempo. Any beat may be elongated to show change in meter, accentuation in a particular word shape, a particular destination, or a need for more energy. We shape text when gesture shows the importance of weighted syllables. This comes by utilizing gestures that have velocity, rather than weight. Weight slows down the music and wears out the conductor.

In *Evoking Sound*, Dr. Jordan speaks of the importance of adding "velocity" instead of weight. We show grouping or direction by a significant pulling gesture but one without weight or added body gesture. When our gesture migrates elsewhere—head, knees or feet—we weaken that for which we hope: a musical product.

Establishing a Trust Level

Careful, diligent, systematic score study reveals what the music is about. Beginning with the large picture and working toward the smallest detail becomes a delightful adventure. Rehearsal is the starting point for an inspired performance. Trusting your singers and players is not abdicating responsibility. Rather, it encourages individual musicianship as well as care for and responsibility to the music.

Your study invites their interest, not just in learning correct pitches, but toward deeper levels of music-making. Not "just the notes," but "where the notes go."

Your study invigorates your rehearsal planning and execution so that the culminating performance is worthy of the music chosen. A last-minute crash course hardly suffices.

Placing trust in the individuals in your ensemble displays a high degree of affection and respect. The chorus does not determine the degree of success attained in a rehearsal, but your consistency in having faith in them will encourage each of them to work to their potential, thus influencing the amount of progress that is made.

Taking time to know the musicians as individuals is a joy. I always move around before rehearsal, greeting singers (even professional instrumentalists!), asking about their days and showing interest in them personally. When discipline is required it is administered privately. No one should be singled out for "abuse," and no one should serve as scapegoat, especially for a conductor's lack of preparation or inherent failings. Conductor tirades are more show than anything else and often a substitute for real knowledge of the score.

Collaborating Is Crucial

Remember that music-making is a collaborative effort and that the conductor alone does not create the musical outcome of a rehearsal or performance. The picture of someone overconducting, flailing, flopping, swaying, bobbing and weaving is well known to all of us. Ask yourself: Do you look away at such times?

When excessive energy is expended in gesture, essential auditing is diminished. When the conductor does all the work, singers or players are not allowed to make their fullest contributions to the process. Ann Howard Jones instructs us to "engage the music-makers." We only engage when we expect our singers to take responsibility for the final product by marking changes in articulation, tempo, dynamics; circling important syllables; and auditing their own individual sound as well as that of the ensemble.

It is a mistake to think that if we expend more effort as a conductor the choir will attain greater and more beautiful results. Thinking that if we do more they will automatically do more is just wrong. Yet, we continue to see pictures of conducting hyperfunction. When I instruct my students to stand still and let the sound come to them, they often feel constricted and unmusical. They cling to the idea that the more they bob and weave, the better the musical product will be.

Preparing for Success

For me, training in two essentials is crucial to an ensemble: First, members learn how to respond to clear, effective gesture; something that has to be taught. Second, members learn how to mark their scores. My singers know that if I ask to see their music it better have marks in it. Woe unto the HBU singer who offers up an unmarked score. Public flogging in the quadrangle will surely follow! "I'll remember" is the watchword for the slothful and unmusical. Beware!

In rehearsal, the ensemble is formed and the music brought to fruition. I love rehearsing almost more than performing!

Too often the true joys of a productive rehearsal are not fully realized because of our inability to overcome the challenges of our particular situation. As conductors, we have no choice but to deal with the limitations placed upon us.

The daily or alternate-day rehearsals in school settings offer adequate rehearsal time but challenge the teacher to find sufficient time for score study and rehearsal planning. This can result in inefficient, unfocused rehearsals at the beginning of preparations for a performance. As the performance draws closer, everyone gets "serious" and crisis-mode sets in. Rehearsals can be overlong and taxing, and conductors can become maniacs. Singers and instrumentalists take the stage in maddening frustration. Are the results exciting? If adrenaline is the key, yes.

In church, the opposite is true. There is abundant time for score study and rehearsal preparation, but never the luxury of too much rehearsal time! The difficulty of rehearsing only once a week with a group of singers whose membership is constantly changing is a challenge which can be daunting.

Time is a valuable commodity in either situation and should not be wasted. We must work quickly and efficiently every single moment we're in contact with our singers. Most of us realize that only when music is in the bones (that is to say: the music has been rehearsed to a point that it saturates one's being) are the results really satisfactory and long lasting. It is up to us to meet the challenges we face so that the end result represents a step-by-step ascension to a higher plane rather than a falling-down-the-stairs experience.

When asked what weaknesses Margaret Hillis saw in young choral conductors, she responded:

> They need to learn to study a score properly and make contact with the sound. Sonority: There is a feeling that the sonority is in your hands and that the music itself goes right by your face. It would be similar to sitting by the source of the sound when you play and having real contact with it.

Some things about conducting cannot be taught. Talent cannot be taught. You cannot really teach group dynamics. There has to be a sense of atmosphere, and you have to know when to move on—when something has been rehearsed enough. I do demand detail, thinking and connecting, but it has to be in the context of the whole.[2]

She continues:

You must stand up straight in rehearsals. Conducting is really the psychology of motion. If your body is open, poised and free when you conduct, you're going to get that kind of sound. If it's tight and closed, your forces aren't going to be able to breathe very well. It is crucial never to tighten up through the chest. As soon as you do that, they begin to follow what you're doing and they have no room to breathe. A music director who sincerely loves music and works with people as fellow human beings all focused on the same things makes conducting as easy as falling off a log. But if it's one of those martinets who whips them over the head, you don't get the same kind of contact.[3]

Applying These Concepts to Repertoire

Two contrasting pieces have been chosen for discussion. One is essentially legato with long lines, while the second is brisk and in multiple meter. The challenge in the legato piece is to pull the phrasal lines forward with precise gesture. That is, singers move off of the exact rhythmic definition seen in the conducting. It is a mistake to think that beautiful legato will happen by swaying or moving about. We show by precise preparatory beats when to start, what vocal quality to use, how loud or soft to sing, and where the musical line is going. Often, as in a Renaissance motet, there are more lines moving than can (or should) be conducted; all the more reason for studying carefully, teaching thoughtfully and contacting the music-makers who, after all, actually sing. You, gentle reader, do not sing!

In the multiple-meter piece, one's command of technique and logical grouping of meter makes an exciting performance possible. The old joke about counting mixed meter as 1-2-3-4-5-6-sev-en is not really all that humorous. Dodging the issue and retreating into vagueness with a sort of added rhythmic smudge is a thin disguise for lack of rhythmic stability.

First Light

Daniel E. Gawthrop
SATB, a cappella
Published by Dunstan House

History

This piece was a commission from Houston Baptist University as a part of a weeklong residency by Mr. Gawthrop. The text is by Jane Griner.

Finding the Sound

This sound does not have an historical reference except perhaps that of a motet or madrigal with intertwining polyphonic lines. A linear piece requires an appropriate sound, more like *O Magnum Mysterium.*

Performance Possibilities/Teaching Strategies

This exquisite text is full of meaning and metaphor. It sings because the music is "in the words." To teach notes without understanding accentuation, phrase length and destination is to have a correct but dull performance.

As one looks at the first excerpt from this piece, with articulation added by this author, the intensity of textual expression is shown by the conductor with tall alignment and precise preparation. Our tendency is to be with them when, in actuality, we must always be ahead of them. We pull lines across, never reaching over into their territory and never attempting to make them sing, which is something we really can't do anyway. Receiving sound that passes right by your face is our job; singing the text is theirs!

One other Yarrington-ism: Consonant articulation makes the legato possible. Singing a beautiful, connected legato requires tremendous diction. The consonants carve a place in the continuous line of sound. Obviously the "m-n-ng" sounds carry their own legato and resonance. The old Fred Waring tone-syllables approach is useful to remember. Imprecise articulation makes for sloppy legato, and sloppiness is *not* next to Godliness.

First Light

SATB chorus *a cappella*

Jane Griner

Daniel E. Gawthrop

Measures 49–58

I Will Sing and Give Praise

Alice Parker
SATB and Soprano Solo with Organ or Piano
Published by Hinshaw Music, Inc.

History

Like the Gawthrop piece, this was a commissioned piece. The occasion was for the dedication of a small two-manual organ. It was written for the organ, SATB choir and a soprano soloist. Parker maintains that a more specific commission is actually freeing, for one knows for whom one is writing.

Finding the Sound

The closest frame of reference would be a psalter hymn with its insistent rhythms and lightness of approach and a sound that approximates a recorder.

Performance Possibilities/Teaching Strategies

Everything you need to know is contained in the introduction to this piece:

> Lightly, playfully ($\quarternote = \quarternote$ throughout)
> $\halfnote = 120$

First, the obvious:
$\frac{4}{4}$ is in 2
$\frac{6}{4}$ is in 2
$\frac{3}{2}$ is in 3
$\frac{3}{4}$ is in 1
$\frac{5}{4}$ is 3 plus 2

The less obvious:
- The 2 of the $\frac{4}{4}$ measure equals two half-notes.
- The 2 of the $\frac{6}{4}$ measure, however, equals two dotted half-notes. In other words: The pattern for the $\frac{4}{4}$ is a simple two. The pattern for the $\frac{6}{4}$ is also in two, but elongated to take in the added quarter notes.
- The 3 of the $\frac{3}{2}$ is simply a large 3 indicating three half-notes.
- The $\frac{5}{4}$ (3 plus 2) is a longer downbeat (for 3) and a shorter beat (for 2).

The quality of these downbeats and upbeats needs to remain light and playful, not heavily beaten. A precise ictus coupled with elongation shows the differing patterns and keeps the playfulness alive.

In speaking about this piece to the conducting class at HBU, Parker said that as she spoke "I will sing … SING … S I N G and give praise," she knew how the music would go. (The music is in the words.) The mixed meter was a result of the textual ideas, not something put in for show or difficulty.

The interplay between soloist and choir is delightful, and there are some exciting and interesting places along the journey. The wise conductor will:

1. Look at the big picture, identifying major sections.
2. Draw a solid bar line down to identify phrase structure and length.
3. Bracket the patterns in various meters.
4. Practice, practice, practice the conducting until it is natural, light, playful, full of nuance, color and sound, and does not get in the way of the music. If you have to think which way you are moving in your pattern, you are not ready to stand before the group.
5. For the choir, lots of speaking (or whispering) of text in rhythm while avoiding a sing-song treatment is a good strategy. Speaking is not punishment but a way to get on board with the textual/musical ideas.

I WILL SING AND GIVE PRAISE

for Mixed Voices, S.A.T.B., Soprano Solo, with Organ or Piano

Adapted from
The Psalms by A. P.

ALICE PARKER

Measures 41–47

Measures 83–88

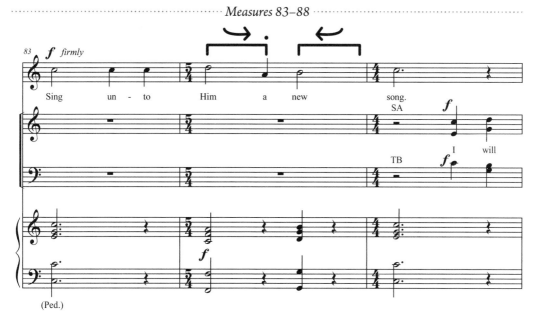

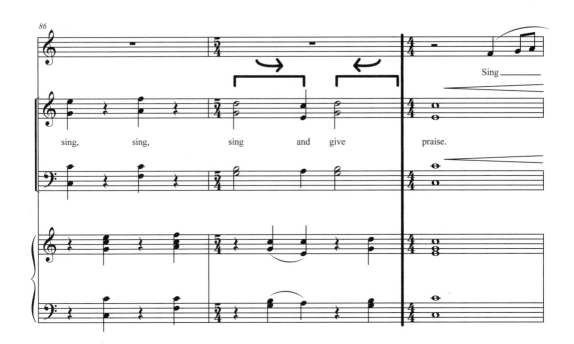

Measures 162–176

Chapter Four

Preparing the Ensemble for the Conversation

No symphony orchestra just sits down and plays. It comes onto the stage, gets settled and begins playing scales, arpeggios and even passages from the upcoming concert. It gets ready to make music. Some choirs use the no-warm-up method: be warmed up when you come so we don't waste time and can get right to the music. I do not subscribe to this method.

The warm-up/tune-up is, of course, not a waste of time. On the contrary, everyone in the room is reminded of why they came, encouraged to limber up physically and aurally, allowed to listen and tune simple chords and scale patterns, encouraged to sing beautiful vowels, and given the opportunity to focus on flexibility and range enhancement.

A runner who starts without proper stretching will hurt himself. We should do no less with our vocalists. In those Carnegie Hall experiences with Robert Shaw, he often took as much as 30 minutes to warm up and tune. This was an intense time that produced results.

In church, a carefully structured five-minute warm-up period is ensemble-creating. Asking everyone in the room to begin with stretching, vocalizing, etc. makes beautiful offerings possible on Sunday mornings. The time is never wasted. Often, parts of familiar hymns or even excerpts from current literature can be incorporated.

We should not sing one way in the warm-up and then discard all of that when we do the "real music." What we accomplish in warming up and in tuning up is crucial to the outcome of the music-making. It can be fun, as in *Sing Legato*.[1] It must be varied, thoughtful, planned and timed. We should give only the briefest direction. A long dissertation on breath support is a waste of time. Ask the members to sing, then listen, encourage and correct, then sing again. Used wisely, five minutes is an enormous amount of time.

Goals and Procedures for Warm-Up/Tune-Up

1. Begin with stretching.

2. Continue with humming and chewing in low, medium and high range.

3. Start in mid-range (E♭ major with B♭ on top; scale steps 5-4-3-2-1; listening, lightening up as you descend). Then, raise the pitch one half-step.

4. Encourage relaxed, *not dropped*, jaw.

5. Encourage upper-register sound that contains light, energetic production.

6. Balance simple warm-up exercises with tuning exercises.

7. Vary the routine.

8. Expect complete attention; don't allow anyone, including yourself, to become preoccupied.

9. Keep what you do simple so the concentration is on the desired effect. Vocalizes that are too complicated never do what we think they will.

10. Work two vowels together: "nee-oh," "nee-ah," "nee-oo," etc.

11. Always work for beauty of sound.

12. Always work for wonderful intonation.

13. Never just "go through the motions."

14. Plan, write down and time your work.

Never, never begin in the key of C major. This only encourages lower-register singing with heavy, weighty production. We should always begin in mid-range (E♭ major) with a five-note descending pattern, then raise the pitch by half-steps. We should stay in mid-range for the first part of the warm-up, gradually increasing the expectation for members to sing higher and lower with good tone production. How will your group learn to sing well throughout their range if you don't offer them a step-by-step process to accomplish this? How will they learn to sing with a wide dynamic range if you don't ask for that in the warm-up?

It is imperative that you know what you want to accomplish with each and every exercise. Sometimes, in the case of register-change exercises (for example, "I love to sing" on 5-8-5-3-1), a simple explanation or demonstration is useful. Mostly, we talk too much during the warm-ups, especially with volunteer church choir members.

Your voice is always your best model. You don't have to be the best singer, but you need to be able to demonstrate all of the color, energy, tone, and beautiful vowel production that you wish them to have when they sing. Listen to what comes back; encourage and correct (don't scold) and repeat, repeat, repeat. In church choirs, some never really catch on. Some come late on purpose to avoid the warm-up. Some come late because that is their habit. Some bring their body with no mind attached. God does work in mysterious ways and, often, something wonderful happens. Nothing wonderful happens if you begin by simply singing the first hymn or anthem without the benefit of any warm-up or tuning exercises.

Vocal Warm-Ups

The exercises that follow are predicated on the idea that singers begin in mid-voice, using more upper-register sound than lower-register sound (or more light mechanism than heavy mechanism). Those who chose to begin in a speaking-voice register with the intent of injecting energy into the sound often find that this creates tuning problems. This is especially true when the singer is descending on a five-note pattern. Helen Kemp always tells singers and conductors, "the lower, the lighter." It helps to ask singers to use both hands in a lifting motion as the pitches descend to avoid having excessive weight in the tone.

In his book *Singing: The Mechanism and the Technic*, William Vennard writes:

> I ask all of my students to do what we call the "yawn-sigh." The exercise is quite informal and should be done as easily and comfortably as possible. It consists simply of simulating a yawn and exhaling gently and vocally. The emotional atmosphere should be happy, relieved. The mood should be of relaxation, like the feeling at the end of a perfect day, "tired but happy."
>
> In order to get the desired relaxation without breathiness, it will be necessary that "head tone" or quasi-falsetto be used. The initial pitch should be one that is comfortably located in the upper part of the range and should glide down into the "chest voice."[2]

The focus should be on achieving a high quality of sound rather than simply producing a large quantity of sound. Ask the singers to listen more than they sing to keep them aware of the goal of each exercise as well as their own progress.

The first warm-up exercise below is based on the Vennard yawn-sigh. Breathe as in the beginning of a yawn with a relaxed jaw, tall vowel, molto legato. Begin in E♭ major with a B♭ on top. Raise the pitch by half-steps but stay within the octave range of E♭ major. Listening as the singers descend, 5-4-3-2-1, is crucial, especially scale step 3, which tends to flat. Say to the singers, "as you inhale, feel cool air in the back of your throat, release (don't drop) the jaw and connect immediately with the breath."

Raise pitch a half step and repeat

Move from the "yah" vowel to two vowels: "yah moh yah moo yah" or "yah may yah mee yah."

Raise pitch a half step and repeat

The next exercise targets the same vocal idea, but with "yah mah yah moh yoo." Take care that repeated notes don't sag in pitch. Avoid this by asking the singers to add a slight bit of energy on each successive repeated pitch before descending.

Raise pitch a half step and repeat

Continue this same vocal idea, using the vowels "yah mah yah may yee."

Raise pitch a half step and repeat

Go immediately to the "ng" with relaxed jaw and then open to "ah," sustain, then descend. Carefully tune each descending pitch. Some people speak of "popping the palate," which may be useful. Ask singers to take one hand, palm up, and gently give a rising gesture as the pitch descends.

Now, go immediately to the "ng," moving immediately into the "ah," and immediately into the "mmm" of "mama." Achieving a feeling or sensation of resonance or "ping" or forward placement without nasality is the desired result. Even though we know resonance is not actually accomplished in the area of the mid-face, we feel it there and that sensation is valuable. This is not a nasal sound, but a tall vowel with raised palate which is focused in the mid-face area.

The following warm-up is all about the breath. "H" is wonderful for freeing the vocal mechanism. Relax the jaw, release on the breath.

In the following warm-up, a quick "bl" into a tall "ah" with relaxed jaw creates a really "blah" attack!

This next warm-up is for registration flexibility. The pickup note on the word "I" is light and moves over the top with a liquid "L." It is important to produce a pure vowel on "love," a pure vowel on "to" and a final pure vowel on "sing."

Tuning is the emphasis of the following warm-up. All sustain the F♯ on "noo," "noh" or "nah." Higher voices (soprano/tenor) move up one half-step; lower voices sustain. Lower voices (alto/bass) move down one half-step; higher voices sustain. All move back to the unison F♯.

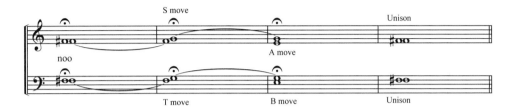

The purpose of the following exercise is for the singers to work on tuning a four-part chord. All sustain the opening pitch on "noo," "noh" or "nah." Ask one part to move while the other three parts sustain.

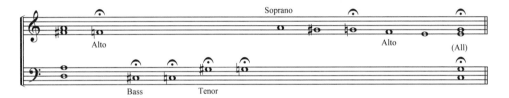

Chapter Five

Rehearsal Is the Lifeblood of the Conversation

Time is a valuable commodity not to be wasted. This is reason enough to carefully plan your rehearsals, but there are others.

The rehearsal should unfold like a symphonic movement, have a culminating point, then taper off. After the warm-up/tune-up, begin with something familiar, transition into the most difficult work and conclude with something more accessible. The result of such a well-paced rehearsal can bring a fulfilling, satisfying sense of completion.

I find it helpful to identify the number of rehearsals before a performance (or Sunday anthem) and outline the plan for each rehearsal. Our goal at HBU, where we're on a 10-week quarter system, is to be concert-ready after the eighth week of the quarter for a concert at the end of the ninth week. On the board the students see, "five weeks before performance," then "four weeks before performance." Posting a performance countdown keeps everyone aware of what remains to be accomplished and the time available to do it. This places the responsibility of being ready on the choir and helps them to avoid falling into the trap of thinking they can pull it out at the last minute.

The need for systematic preparation is equally important to school, community and church choirs. Those of us in church know how important it is to constantly encourage readiness. In school, there is more time for rehearsal, but the literature is usually more difficult and challenging. This is all the more reason to work steadily toward the goal, thereby negating the call for extra rehearsals and that last-minute panic, which succeeds only in making choristers nervous. Substantial musical performance can occur only when the music is learned well, and that requires careful planning and relentless rehearsing.

Every rehearsal plan should have variety. Sometimes it is helpful to sing through a piece without stopping to give everyone an idea of its readiness. Again, we should place responsibility on the choristers to be aware of their individual progress and to have a clear idea of what remains to be done.

Though this seems obvious, we should know how long a particular piece (or large work) is or how long our program of several selections is. We should not plan more than we can accomplish in any given rehearsal, especially in a longer work. Counting the cost in terms of time is essential. Hurrying through a rehearsal without foundation is tantamount to disaster.

The Introduction

The manner in which a new piece is introduced has a great influence on how well performance preparation goes, as well as on the degree of quality achieved in the performance. The conductor must know the essential musical elements and, from the beginning, interest singers in the unique qualities of the piece.

As the choir is introduced to unfamiliar music, establish a hospitable and receptive atmosphere. "Hospitality doesn't make painful things less painful but makes painful things possible." Encourage your singers to keep an open mind as new pieces are presented, and let them know it's all right to voice their opinions. Just as a hospitable person is warm and accepting, so should they give each new piece the benefit of the doubt. But remember, while everyone has a right to an opinion, the rehearsal cannot turn into a free-for-all. The negative voice is, after all, the strongest, both in church and in school. Take care not to let the naysayers dominate.

"I know what I like" usually means, "I like what I know." This attitude, prevalent in church-choir mentality, also manifests itself at school where the comfort zone is usually not too far ranging. Our job is to patiently and persistently bring everything we know to enhance understanding and appreciation of whatever work is to be sung. We all have experienced the following: "I used to dislike that Vaughan Williams "Hodie," but now I love it!" This is high praise for both the work and for your careful and stubborn championing of its right to be sung.

This approach is called establishing the "want to." The goal is to generate enthusiasm while the singers greet a new piece and accept its challenges. Regardless of the piece's style, I almost always begin with speaking the text. Speaking all parts together rhythmically and musically is a good beginning exercise.

Varied Approaches

The following techniques speed the rehearsal onward and enable the learning:

- Singing on neutral syllables
- Count-singing
- Singing text on a four-part chordal ostinato
- Using solfége with hand signals
- Combining singing and speaking

Sometimes a before-and-after approach works as singers are invited to contrast different stylistic practices. On the Haydn, for instance, one might say: "sing this like it is a major work by Brahms, molto legato and very connected. Now, again, this time with lighter, more focused tone, more like a Haydn quartet and less like a tuba ensemble."

Identifying potential trouble spots when you are studying the score is helpful in planning rehearsals, but you should be willing to take what comes for free. Celebrate those moments when the choir skillfully handles a passage you thought would require extra work.

After some time with a piece, scrambling parts can be extremely beneficial. Singers can confirm what they know and discover where they are insecure. Listening is enhanced when singers are in mixed formation. What the singer can hear when surrounded by other parts can lead to improved tuning, blend and balance.

Rehearsing is teaching: show where the seams are; circle difficult pitches; circle entrances, especially those that are unprepared. Teach singers what to listen for and where careful listening is most essential. Help them understand what voice or voices are most important in the texture. Mr. Shaw marked *soli* in many scores to indicate primary material. When dealing with accompanied music, identify what instruments are playing and which pitches are given by clarinet, violin, etc. Using a recording, especially with less experienced singers, provides a concept of the whole.

The three Rs of rehearsal are, of course, repeat, repeat, repeat! Though I would extend that to repeat with much variety and positive reinforcement of what is good, and with less scolding, less talking, more singing, and more listening.

A Rehearsal Credo

1. From the start, use tall vowels and crisp consonants and work for beauty of sound.

2. Interest singers in the beauty of text. Speak text for word shapes, inflection, direction and destination. Make sense of the text by dealing with thoughts and ideas (represented by phrases).

3. Be musical at all times during the learning process.

4. Help singers identify and understand the structure of a piece. Locate sections or divisions, repeated places and patterns. Form is a great teacher.

5. Encourage a wide range of dynamics, especially an energized soft sound.

6. Teach singers to circle accent syllables, draw arrows up to indicate a need for better intonation, draw arrows down over important words or phrasal destinations, underline change of syllable, mark quick page turns, and circle difficult places. Placing visual cues in the score is essential, and pencils are a necessary part of the rehearsal.

Performance

Prevalent in church and in school to a lesser extent is the notion that we do not "perform." In church, performance might have a bad connotation. Roger Deschner gives his perspective in *Your Ministry of Singing in the Church Choir*:

> An ill-thought cliché has been on the lips of many church musicians. They say our choirs do not "perform." To them, performance is a bad word. "Performers" are people who act out parts (whether they believe [them] or not) for personal accolades. Although we are all tempted to play that part, it is the very opposite of what we are called to be and do in our tradition. The problem is that "performance" at root has never had that crass meaning. We need the word when talking about church music. God uses the word in making demands on our choirs. It must be salvaged. If we are talking about "selfish uses of church music," then that's what we should say. That temptation to misuse church music must always be held to the light. God asks us today in our choirs, as God has always asked, that we give—let loose of—offer—our best "performance" that we have carefully prepared for God's use.

> Performance simply means to complete what one has set out to do and to accomplish it with the special skills required. Performance asks us to take the time to complete thorough preparations. Performance asks us to hone our

skills. Performance demands commitment, time, work and a willingness to use our talents. The opposite of good performance is half-done, half-learned, misunderstood, shoddy, rag-tag offerings of music.[1]

Likewise, at school, we have no business standing on a riser or stepping on the podium if we have not let loose of ourselves in the service of the music. I tell aspiring conductors that everyone knows immediately if they have done their work, especially if an orchestra is present. You simply cannot fake it. Your careful study is what makes an inspiring performance possible.

Chapter Six
What Do They Need for the Conversation?

In *Reprise*, the Alabama state newsletter for ACDA, Edna Clay writes an intriguing article entitled "Learning Styles" in which she advocates understanding the "individual uniqueness" of the individual singer.

> Even though diversity of talents, ideas and values are more demanding, the variety in our world is what makes it exciting and adventurous. Being able to keep our individual uniqueness while yet being part of a community is a challenge. We as choral conductors have the joy of helping individuals share and blend talents with the goal of providing opportunity for singers to be intellectually and emotionally stimulating and stimulated.[1]

She asks, "What is an outstanding choral group?" Her answer: "a group of individuals who work so well together that they become one in spirit." What a great definition of purpose for our work! In discussing the many ways one "encodes" information, Clay outlines a preferred sense or style of learning as follows:

Visual learners need few words, are appearance-oriented and desire eye contact. Terms used by visuals include see, clearly, perspective, bright/dim, horizon, view, look, blind, stare, focus, outlook, foggy.

Auditory learners love the language of words. They learn best by hearing. They can be as confused by pictures as the visual are confused by words. Auditories can mimic sounds and are wonderful with languages. Auditories respond to words of praise. Predicates and phrases which they like and use include hear, talk, listen, loud, soft, sounds like, clear, ring a bell, tone, say, repeat.

Kinesthetic learners like to feel the music. They learn by doing. Kinesthetics are strongly intuitive and sometimes let feelings interfere with the fine-tuning of a performance. They just want to open their mouths and sing! (Sounds like many a church choir singer I have directed.)

In summary, Clay gives this advice: "In teaching a vocal technique, you will want to show the visuals, tell the auditories and explain to the kinesthetics what the feelings are, both internal and external."

Sally Herman makes these telling comments in *In Search of Musical Excellence*:

> In the classroom, most of us are going to teach in a manner compatible with our own learning style because of the security that allows us. We tend to think that because we understand a concept best if presented in a certain manner, so will our students. Only if we have a clear picture of the diversity with which individuals perceive things can we begin to find methods to accommodate those differences.[2]

Herman, a master teacher whom I have seen applying this concept very effectively, refers to *Please Understand Me* by David Keirsey and Marilyn Bates as a wonderful resource for understanding how people learn.[3]

When I think of all the years I have spent working with volunteer singers in church, I realize how important learning styles are. Some of my major frustration has been a result of my lack of understanding of how others process information. It is not that different in my present school environment. The more we understand about styles of learning, the more effective our teaching will become.

So, the question is: What do they need?

What do they need?

...To Accommodate Various Learning Styles

- *Visual learners:* few words, eye contact, conducting gesture that is clear and compelling.
- *Auditory learners:* words of praise, hearing the anthem all the way through, using my voice as the best model for what I want.
- *Kinesthetic learners:* tracing a phrase physically, pointing to a climactic place, and having them conduct with appropriate gesture.

I realize that I use combinations of all of these to get results. This is all the more reason for such emphasis on score study, as is frees me from the page so that I might observe behavior and change and adapt during a rehearsal. The temptation is to blame, scold and take out one's frustration on the singers rather than adjust, adapt and be aware of the dynamics of a particular rehearsal. Anyone can say: "Sopranos, you are flat!" The master teacher realizes this and makes suggestions in a positive way to reinforce the desired outcome.

...In Church

Singers need The Security Factor. They need and want extensive repetition on the music. Sectionals are valuable but only if musical understanding is always present. Learning correct pitches without knowing where they go or who goes with them is a waste of time. Usually, two parts in a sectional work better because there is always interplay and understanding.

Establishing routines for the robe, music and seating issues speaks directly to their security. Reviewing choreography (sitting, standing, holding folders, etc.) does as well.

Such simple changes as different music for Doxology, Gloria and Lord's Prayer, word substitutions in hymns or anthems, singing from the balcony or in the aisles, or processing to a different side of the chancel are all changes that speak to their security. We help our people adapt to The Change Factor as best we can, knowing all the while that when we write instructions on the board someone will have a question.

> On the board: Movement one - be seated.
> Question: "Do we sit while we sing during movement one?"

> Sign above list of music: Tonight's music.
> Question: "Is this tonight's music?"

> Instruction: Please hum the tonic or home note.
> Question: "Are we going to hum downstairs in the chancel?"

Anyone who has ever directed a volunteer choir knows I speak the truth. We attempt to honor traditional ways as much as possible. We endeavor to be hospitable to those incredibly thoughtless questions. (I don't do this well, I confess.) However, we hope to foster an atmosphere of hospitality. Often something new is suspect simply because it is out of the comfort zone. Time works wonders. The choir members are not going to like all of the choices of anthems, responses or hymns. A short explanation (with absence of defensiveness) can help, but the negative voice is always the strongest. If we have chosen well and appropriately, we can ride out these squalls.

...In School

Generally, the literature in school is more difficult and there is more of it than for a church choir. Too often, a year's repertoire is planned with little regard to providing exposure to what we might consider standard choral literature. Ideally, in a four-year cycle we introduce, teach and perform a wide variety of the most outstanding pieces of many different style periods.

I find The Change Factor to be an issue in college just as it is in church. Most of my students have a comfort level from late Renaissance to Romantic. We are farthest apart in time from early music on the one hand and contemporary music on the other. Interestingly enough, I found in performing a program of spirituals that I needed to do a lot of educating on this particular style. Many students didn't understand the history nor the performance practices contained therein. Moreover, the snobs (mostly music majors) felt this music was somehow beneath them. As with any style, generating an understanding of historical place and performance practices is the best approach.

In school, The Security Factor is as prevalent as in church. Positive reinforcement in the beginning stages is a must. Our careful score study reveals where and how we begin and dictates the pace of learning. Without that, we and they are flying blind. The danger in school is that there is more time and it can easily be wasted. Then, as mentioned earlier, there is that last-minute crunch time before performance. It doesn't have to happen this way.

...In Both Church and School

The Care Factor speaks volumes. Not to care individually about your singers, not to know them by name, not to welcome them at each rehearsal means, to me, that the music is almighty but the music-makers can come and go.

I am prepared for each rehearsal with a written plan so I am not at the stand working when they come in. I can greet them, ask them about their day, be sensitive to that one who needs a bit of extra TLC. Nothing is as sweet as the sound of one's own name.

With professional orchestras I always make out a seating chart with names of the players so when I ask for more Oboe II, I call that player by name. Often, after working in a city for a time, one knows the players and can greet them during the pre-rehearsal time.

While I value e-mail, I find that an individual note or card is substantially better. We all love to get a personal note, which takes no more time than firing up the computer. When I send out mimeographed notices or cards I always append a personal note, if only one sentence. Recently, at a rehearsal, a former youth choir member, now a grown man with children of his own, showed me a card I had sent him with a personal note. He had saved that card all these years.

My friend David McKechnie, a Presbyterian pastor, tells the story of sending out Christmas cards to members of his parish, signing them while thinking about other things. A woman came up to thank him for her card. "It was no big deal," replied Pastor McKechnie. "You don't understand," she said. "It was the only card I received." After that, the signing and sending of cards took on a whole new meaning for him.

As Director of the School of Music at Houston Baptist University, I know our students and faculty. They know that I am available to them, that I am trustworthy and that I care. I arrive early each day to get the mundane out of the way so I can always stop when someone comes in. Too accessible, you say. It's all about accessibility, I say.

Chapter Seven
What Do I Need for the Conversation?

I have tried to be clear about what "they" need whether in school or at church. I know, however, that what I need is equally as important. I am first and foremost a teacher, utilizing all the gifts I have, which include recognizing differing learning styles, studying and practicing constantly, and preparing carefully for every rehearsal, but, as the scriptures say, "the greatest of these is love."

I love the people I conduct, and I need their love in return. Nothing is as satisfying to me as looking over an ensemble made up of individuals, knowing their frailty—knowing *my* frailty—and being in the center of the action. The podium is a dangerous place. Everything, both good and bad, is revealed. I am never as good as I want to be, and I continuously compare myself to others, which is, of course, fruitless. I often ask myself, "Whose idea was this?" Even after all these years, those first moments with a new ensemble or that first rehearsal with the chorus and orchestra cause me inner turmoil. I prepare in order to get through those first minutes. After that, I am all right.

I have learned that to trust one's instincts is a good thing, for instinct that is based on careful study and experience in differing styles succeeds. If one is not convinced about decisions regarding voicing, instrumentation and performance practice, and if one has not carefully rehearsed, the results may prove disastrous.

Can love for the music and the music-makers co-exist with the highest of expectations and the necessity of staying on task? I believe it can. Am I sensitive to the body languages of my group? Certainly! Does it ever bother me? All the time! Those basses in your church choir, with arms crossed in front of their chests, are not saying: "Gee, we're glad you went to that workshop and came back with some new music and new ideas." Not at all! But, I am a teacher who loves the music and the music-makers, so I find a way that works for me. I am at my best when the best "me" I know is on that podium, loving the product, encouraging the singers and players, and realizing what a great privilege it is to be there.

What do I need, then:

1. **Constant meditation and prayer.** I begin every day with scripture and prayer and with a specific list of those for whom I pray. I arrive early at my office, and this is the first order of business.

2. **Collegiality.** We must all work with others, be it those on a church staff or in our own music departments. Some relationships are easier to establish than others. I enjoy learning what others do in their jobs and try to respect them, particularly in regards to scheduling. Taking the youth choir out over a weekend when a youth rally or camp has been scheduled doesn't work. In fact, most conflicts arise over issues of scheduling. Being a part of the solution rather than part of the problem is important. Knowing that a student in your "top" choir has a recital in the evening and excusing her from the rehearsal that day is a gesture sure to reap rewards. The choral department and the rest of the church staff need not be in conflict but, all too often, the music department in church or the choral department in a school is the "war" department. Avoid this by allowing for give and take when scheduling. I also need a colleague whom I trust with my very life and from whom I hold back nothing. I need to be able to pick up the phone and say whatever is on my mind, whatever is troubling me. This colleague also enjoys equal privilege. How does one get along without a friend willing to listen and tell the truth in love? I am fortunate in this.

3. **Positive reinforcement.** Just as I believe in being an encourager, I also need encouragement. I am always amazed that students or choir members are aware that something is wrong in my life and are there with a word or a card. A note, call or e-mail from a colleague taking notice of good work is always appreciated. I believe all of us need an "atta-boy."

4. **Lessons from others.** Constant reading of new books and periodicals, attendance at workshop events and asking questions means I am functioning at a good level. I am never afraid to ask or to try a new approach.

5. **A project.** Whether a large score to study, language diction to improve, a new language to learn or a book to write, I need to be working on something.

6. **Distance from the comparison game.** I am fortunate to have rubbed shoulders with some of the best in our business, and it is very difficult for me not to make comparisons. At First Methodist Dallas, we always brought in a clinician to work the summer

workshop, and it always seemed to me that every note that person touched turned to gold. I found myself thinking, "I say the very same thing but without the result." After the second rehearsal, I would be depressed because I was in the comparison game. The truth is that I wanted my folks to work with the very best person available. One might say I set myself up for comparison year after year. On the other hand, after I relaxed, I learned volumes. At HBU we have an artist-in-residence every year, usually a composer whose music we perform at the end of the week. I remember looking over at Morten Lauridsen before the first rehearsal with the choirs on his music and thinking, "Whose great idea was this?" Lauridsen was wonderful, of course, and what composer doesn't want his music performed and, hopefully, performed well?

In *Remembering Robert Lawson Shaw*, Alice Parker writes:

What did I learn? There's no holding back—throw yourself in without counting the cost or time. Be your own harshest critic. (I was never as good as Mr. Shaw at this.) Listen all the time: the specific word, accent, mouth, voice, person, composer. Capture the sound on the page. In the last analysis (and the first), one can't separate the text, the melody and the setting: it's all one. In study and rehearsal, one pulls them apart but only to reunite them.

I learned that the spirit is in the details. That sharing ideas, bouncing them back and forth is enormous fun, stimulating both players to greater achievement. That almost anything can be improved. That one is always walking a delicate balance-line between thought and action, intuition and craft, work and play, rehearsal and performance, life and art. And, that music is one of the greatest gifts and sternest masters. When we enter its world we must submerge our individuality in its surge and ebb, only finding our own voice through the mastery of its demands.[1]

Chapter Eight
When In Our Music

When in our music God is glorified,
And adoration leaves no room for pride,
It is as though the whole creation cried: Alleluia![1]

—F. Pratt Green

No Room for Pride

On a recent trip to China, I found new Christians hungry for the Gospel and needing many more pastors or lay leaders. Bible schools are springing up all over the country where people 18 to 35 years old come for one, two or three years of study and then return to their local congregations.

I visited one such school started by a pastor who had been imprisoned for 10 years during the cultural revolution. When he was released, he came out, prayed and started a bible school in a field. Thanks to his efforts, it has prospered. He prays for only what he needs—nothing more—and receives. Now the government is actually going to contribute money for a new building. Students live eight to a small room, hanging their clothes from the ceiling to dry. They have two outfits, one formal and one casual. "No room for pride." When I think about this kind of commitment and sacrifice, comparing it to my own Christian walk, I am brought up short. What have I sacrificed? Not really very much.

I can learn, however, and dedicate myself anew to my work at school and church. And I can call others to renewed dedication and study. For instance, where did we get the idea that we will be led to do this or that without any study or experience? I love the statement: God calls the qualified and qualifies the call.

At HBU, students who are adept at leading worship in a praise-and-worship style come to see me. One will say, "God called me last night and told me that I don't need to study music history or theory to be a music director in a church." I am tempted to reply, "I believe it was a wrong number." I believe in "call," but one built upon individual gifts and graces and qualified with study and diligence.

I remember the singer at a church rally who spoke about the song he was to sing. He told us that God had given him this song. He proceeded to sing, not very well, and actually stopped at least once. When he finished, a lady across the table said, "Wasn't it wonderful that the Lord led him to sing that song." I replied, as my wife was tugging on my sleeve, "Wouldn't it have been wonderful if the Lord had led him to *learn* it?" For me, no room for pride means:

- I have the responsibility of choice, which I take seriously. But it is not easy. The question "when will you do the Verdi *Requiem*?" is put to me quite frequently at HBU and First Presbyterian. My answer is always the same: "never." We simply don't have the forces for that piece at either place. The height of pride would be not to recognize the obvious. To choose the Verdi would be not about the work or the singers, but about me.

- Choosing is difficult. We sang the Ferguson arrangement of "Lord of the Dance" for Easter, and there is a dramatic speaking part in the middle.[2] This fell out of the comfort zone for several Presbyterian choir members. I had to be sure in my own mind that I had chosen this piece for its appropriate text and intriguing setting, and to go ahead in spite of the vote of some choir members. Make no mistake about it: They do vote. Sometimes subtly, sometimes not. My problem of pride is that I want all of them to like all of my choices and to ratify them with their approval, which almost never happens, totally. When they don't, I have a tendency to become sarcastic toward them out of anger. This is motivated by pride more than anything else.

- Believing in a choice means I am willing to stay the course. I have faith in the piece and faith in them. Often it takes a while and requires numerous repetitions. The truth is that not everyone is going to like every choice, no matter how carefully made or winningly presented. Some of them will always be uncomfortable with the unknown (The Fear Factor) but we can help them grow. On the more difficult choices, their lack of ability gets in the way of their judgment. Something easily achieved is usually not worth very much. So, we stay with it, and often, they will change their opinion.

- Challenge is necessary; there is no growth without it. My study enables creative teaching and rehearsing. My patience gives time for the piece to work its magic on the singer.

- "Just a hymn" is a phrase that causes my blood pressure to rise. We have a treasure trove in a denominational hymnal and often can use something directly out of the book, devising a simple introduction and varying the voicing of the verses. I remember the woman who remarked, "If you are just doing a hymn, I shall stay home." I believe we have an obligation to be creative with our hymnal in anthem and response, and to help our choir members see and appreciate its value.

Hymn Singing

In the preface to *The Voice of Our Congregation: Seeking and Celebrating God's Song for Us,* by Terry York and David Bolin, the authors state:

> Congregations have a voice, a corporate, unified voice, no matter how many opinions are expressed on any given issue. The voice has a message. It is the gospel and the truth that the gospel can be lived out in community. The voice has a mission. It is to whisper, shout, speak and sing the message in daily conversation, times of need and times of worship.
>
> As any pastor knows, musical style is perhaps the biggest deal driving people's emotional response to worship. Many churches are a maelstrom of musical tastes, personality types and worship preferences. In an era of cultural diversity, how can one church find and develop its own authentic voice? With so many opinions available and so many individual preferences, how do we decide what will be our accent?[3]

Garth Bolinder offers food for thought in "Finding Your Worship Voice:"

> The congregation's voice is often, if not most often, expressed in song. Finding songs that "fit" the congregation's voice is very closely associated with finding the voice itself. Their song must express their heart and soul. Their song must "fit," it must be authentic.[4]

For me, the "fit" and the authenticity means careful choice, winning presentation and humility. Here is my checklist the ultimate congregation song—the hymn:

1. The hymns are for the congregation, not the choir or the organist.
2. The choir's main role in worship is to be the congregational song leader. Everything else is secondary.
3. The same attention to word shape, prosody, style, color, and articulation in anthem preparation should carry over into hymn singing. (Unfortunately, choirs and congregations have been allowed to sing hymns in a bland, inarticulate style with no attention to phrase, important

words or different emphases in different verses. As Erik Routley once remarked, "Hymn singing is an unthinking habit.")

4. Find ways and times to use hymns: hymn sings, hymn-of-the-month, church meetings, Sunday school classes, vacation Bible school.

5. Trust the hymn. Don't give much information *about* the hymn. Sing it to them; ask them to sing back. Make it an enjoyable experience. Never attempt to lift them up. The pejorative notion is not what we are about. (No room for pride.)

6. "Unfamiliar" is such a good term, far preferable to "new" or "old," and most certainly to "bad" or "good."

7. Repetition is key. Use the same unfamiliar hymn (even one verse) for all the Sundays in Advent, for instance. Remember, your choir members and your congregation often miss a Sunday.

8. Hold the hymnal. Don't print words in the bulletin. While it is true that many in your congregation don't read music, they can see notes going up or down or staying the same. There is much information contained on the pages. Music notation is a gift passed down through the ages. Don't deprive your church members of the opportunity to benefit from it.

9. All of those hymnal pages look the same, but, of course, they are not. Use knowledge of style and performance practice to differentiate between a hymn like "Holy, Holy, Holy" and "Come Thou Almighty King." (See Parker, *Creative Hymn Singing*.)

10. Encourage your organist to play each verse differently and to lift hands and feet for punctuation. People must breathe, and we supply that punctuation. To play every verse of every hymn as if it is the same is to deny the efficacy of text, which is, after all, what constitutes a hymn. My rule of thumb is the question: "For whom are the hymns." Organist? (no) Choir Director? (no) Pastor? (no) Congregation? (Resounding *yes!*)

So has the church in liturgy and song,
In faith and love, through centuries of wrong,
Borne witness to the truth in every tongue? Alleluia!

Our world is experiencing a hymnic explosion. Exposure to ethnic material gives all of us a global view. I brought back from my China trip a bilingual hymnal in Chinese and English. Many of the hymns we sang with the people are familiar hymns to us, though not in the Chinese language. Much material in contemporary hymnals represents this global view, though it's not always embraced by the congregation. In the 1964 Methodist hymnal, "Holy, Holy, Holy" is printed in English and also in Spanish ("Santo, Santo, Santo") which one member of a Sunday school class found very strange, saying, "I don't know why we should have a hymn in this book in Spanish." Why, indeed?

We Westerners tend to be smug and complacent regarding language. To be in a country where a number of people's "broken English" was much better than my "non-Chinese" is a valuable, if painful, reminder that we should shed our vanity and embrace our brothers and sisters in other lands who speak and sing in other languages.

At St. Paul's Church in Nanging, we sang "Jesu, Jesu," the Ghanaian folk song. We sang in English, but the congregation of Chinese Christians joined in on the refrain spontaneously. It was a moving experience. It was here that the hymns for the day were rehearsed before the service. The singing was powerful, robust and full of heart and meaning. This was good because the pianist and piano gave little encouragement. Think of our sanctuaries in the United States, blessed with organs, pianos and all manner of instruments and sound equipment. Now bring to mind the sometimes listless singing of our congregations. Might it be that we have not paid much of a sacrifice to sing and be present?

Allow me to quote my poem first published in *Somebody's Got My Hymnal!*

> The people who come through your doors at the church,
> Are seeking a life-way, for they're on a search;
> For meaning, for substance, for health-filling fare,
> "To seek a King"—that's why they are there.
>
> Now junk food is tasty and easy to swallow,
> But too much that's sugary can cause one to wallow;
> In unwanted fat, getting bigger, not better,
> So here, dear reader, is Uncle John's Letter.
>
> To you who must choose what your people will sing,
> I beg for balance;
> For to them we bring the widest and best of our hymn-singing treasure,
> As new songs and old songs will bring more than pleasure;
> They satisfy hunger with food that is lasting,
> So on to the banquet where no one is fasting.[5]

A marvelous book is *The Singing Thing: A Case for Congregational Singing* by John L. Bell. He speaks of three kinds of ambiguity in communication:

1. **Musical Ambiguity:** That is, different aspects of sound that produce in us positive, negative or ambivalent resonances; the instrument or voice articulating the music, the style of the music or any discernible tune.

2. **The Tune:** Tunes carry with them memories from the past—from where we were when we first heard this piece, who was playing it or whether it was a good experience. Our ears are not neutral.

3. **Textual Ambiguity:** When we read words, we never do so neutrally, but color their contemporary meanings through their past significance in our lives. Language is a powerful tool for controlling or liberating people. In the song of the church, it can include, exclude or antagonize.[6]

And did not Jesus sing a psalm that night
When utmost evil strove against the light!
Then let us sing, for whom he won the fight, Alleluia!

"The Devil made me do it"

The Devil made me do it—an oft-stated phrase that gets us off the hook regarding our decisions in life. Even Jesus wanted the cup to pass ("not my will but thine"). My evil is seldom of the death-defying type. More times than not it takes the form of:

1. Comparison with others who have place, position, status, and different gifts and graces.

2. Actions—consequences. Like Paul, I do that which I don't want to do. Some consequences are more severe than others, but consequences there are!

3. Not enough faith. Elaine Brown's injunction was: "don't mean well feebly." After the China trip, I vow to return in the summer and teach music in one of those bible schools. I also plan to start to learn Chinese. We shall see!

Looking at today's church, I wonder if it affects the culture or if the culture affects the church. In Evangelism, we seem to be moving toward allowing almost anything in the name of gaining new members. "They" don't know the Lord's Prayer; "they" don't know the Apostles' Creed; "they" don't know that hymn.

Where is our responsibility to teach in a winsome way the tenants, the liturgy, the songs of our faith? Can we balance our desire to win souls for Christ with a witness to what we are losing by the way we are doing it? Jesus "won the fight." I wonder if we put up much of one at all.

Often we take our presence and our money elsewhere. We don't like the preacher. The children's or youth programs are not strong. The choir sings those dreary anthems, and the parking is atrocious. It is a shopping mentality. We debate motives, not ideas, and we impugn our brothers and sisters in Christ, particularly if they respond differently than we do. We beat up people with scripture instead of lifting them up. If someone looks at many of our present-day congregations, they might wonder why anyone would want to be a part of this atmosphere.

On the other hand, an atmosphere of hospitality allows much variety in liturgy, sermons and songs. We should foster and encourage differing styles and approaches. We should be careful not to let our own prejudices get in the way of what is meaningful to someone else.

Does this mean guitars in church? Liturgical dance in church? Passing the peace in church? If we could ever lose our judgmental attitudes on what is appropriate for a particular season or setting, we would be on our way to a more hospitable atmosphere. The church is a learning community. We should foster a learning climate and be willing to open the doors to much that doesn't personally move us. Are we in a fight these days? You bet we are! Are we winning? What *is* winning?

Music and the Arts in the Church

1. Don't compare yourself with others. Find your song and sing it.

2. Be hospitable. Foster an open community where dance, drama and differing points of view can be shared in a loving environment.

3. Speak the truth in love. Some of the most inhospitable behavior may be in church, such as in meetings where the agenda is under the table and real decisions are made not in public but in those places where we gossip about others—in hallways or over the phone, what Avery and Marsh call the "Holy-Hotline." We are often quick to judge without knowing much about the person or behavior exhibited. I don't believe the judging is up to us.

4. Develop a learning community where the tenants of the faith are lovingly embraced and taught.

5. Balance the musical fare in hymn and anthems. Help others learn to embrace the unfamiliar without talking down to them or attempting to lift them up. Raising someone's standards, after all, usually only succeeds in raising their hackles. Teach expectantly and expect learning to occur. Overlook the naysayers; ye shall always have them with you.

6. Fight fair. Sit lightly to oneself. Laugh much, particularly at one's own foibles and shortcomings. Give others some room.

7. Be reconciled to one another in love, charity and openness.

8. Always remember: "I was blind, but now I see."

Let every instrument be tuned for Praise!
Let all rejoice who have a voice to raise!
And may God give us faith to sing always: Alleluia!

What does it mean to be "in tune?" A dictionary definition is: "state of being in the proper pitch; to be in tune, agreement in pitch; unison; harmony." Or, this definition: "frame of mind; mood, accord." And this interesting turn: "tune in to adjust a radio so as to receive signals. Tune out to adjust a radio so as to avoid the signals of a sending station."

You know where I'm going, don't you? How often does someone "tune out" an instruction, an annoying friend or choir member, or an unfamiliar tune or anthem?

Being "in tune" means, to me, that sympathetic, hospitable stance where much is welcomed if not always agreed with or appreciated. There is certainly the accurate tuning of the choir (singing in tune), which is crucial and that aspect is discussed in an earlier chapter. That one can sing, however, without adequately being "in tune" with others is demonstrated on a daily basis. Moreover, those individuals in your ensemble with attitudes and manners that are "out of tune" do harm in very tangible ways.

If we are "tuned for praise" it is not about us! The heartbeat of any ensemble is built on community (see the earlier Parker quote on page 86). It is the togetherness that makes the product more than just right notes and beautiful sounds. Ensemble, after all, means together. It is what we all do *together* that makes the difference. The inner gyro is most evident even to the casual observer.

If we are to achieve this ideal, director and members alike must work constantly for it. "I just can't sit next to so and so" is a frequently heard complaint. "Mary sings without rehearsing and doesn't even come to the warm-up." "Bob smells very bad most of the time." "Gladys wears that awful perfume, and it shuts down my voice." Sound familiar? As much as possible, minor irritations can certainly be addressed privately. The bigger issues need to be aired in a positive but firm manner. Choir officers can be most helpful in this regard.

I like to send around a letter commenting on past rehearsals and lifting up matters of general concern. Mr. Shaw did this regularly, and these "Dear People" letters, published in the book of the same name, are sources of interest and amusement. One can remind and instruct in a manner that gives no individual offense. If mailed, a personal note might give individual encouragement, express concern over personal problems, or, in some cases, remind an individual of his/her responsibilities to the entire group. Blasting the entire choir seldom brings desired results.

What voice do you raise? Is it a voice of hope, expectancy, joy, promise or the strident voice of gossip and hateful commenting? Can you raise your voice in love and purpose, building up those around you, without sacrificing your own personal standards of social and musical excellence? Certainly!

What about the voice of Grace? We certainly want that voice extended to us. How we offer this gift to others is an important discussion. This is not to espouse lack of judgment, standard or principle. Rather it is to be open, receptive and willing to allow others to experience that which for them might be particularly meaningful.

You do not know who sits next to you in the pew. Not everyone had a wonderful childhood. The person next to you may be fighting a powerful addiction or a debilitating depression. Children may be out of control, an older parent may be experiencing the difficulties of advancing age. Often, we really don't know what is going on, but we have a sense that all is not well. Without prying or violating another's space, we can be sympathetic. Just as a family is out of tune when one member suffers, so a choir is the same, because a choir *is* family.

I believe that God gives us faith to sing an always-Alleluia regardless of circumstance. I believe God gives us faith to face the most unfaithful circumstances while we continue to sing that Alleluia. When your heart is breaking over trouble at home or at work; when one of your kids takes the car and runs off with his girlfriend; when your significant other proves unfaithful, we still can and should sing Alleluia. God gives us this song. It is ours to sing faithfully.

Biographical Information of Selected Choral Composers and Conductors

Richard K. Avery

Richard K. Avery was the pastor at First Presbyterian Church in Port Jervis, New York, for 40 years and has retired to Santa Fe, New Mexico. The team of Avery and Marsh (Richard K. Avery and Donald S. Marsh) became widely known throughout the United States and Europe for workshop presentations on creative worship and music and for its publications with Hope Publishing Company.

Elaine Brown

Elaine Brown served on the faculty at Temple University from 1945 to 1956. She garnered countless honors for her achievements in music as well as her humanitarian efforts, and was also the first American woman to conduct the Philadelphia Orchestra. She established the nonprofit Singing City in 1948 and continued to nurture and develop the influence of the group in the community until her retirement in 1987.

John Ferguson

John Ferguson has earned national recognition for his accomplishments as a performer and teacher in the church music field, as well as an organ improviser and leader of congregational singing. Ferguson is an author and composer and travels extensively presenting hymn festivals for local congregations and professional meetings of church musicians. Ferguson is the Elliot and Klara Stockdahl Johnson Professor of Organ and Church Music and Minister of Music to the Student Congregation at St. Olaf College in Northfield, Minnesota.

Daniel E. Gawthrop

Daniel E. Gawthrop is a prolific American composer whose works have been performed in the country's finest concert halls and recorded by leading professional and educational ensembles. He has been commissioned by more than

100 performing ensembles and professional organizations, including the Raymond Brock Memorial series of the American Choral Directors Association.

Julius Herford

Julius Herford taught several generations of choral conductors at Indiana University, including Robert Shaw. He brought rare insight into music's history, construction and performance practice to analysis. His careful, almost tyrannical, attention to detail made possible a new standard for choral and choral/orchestral work in this country.

Jan Harrington

Jan Harrington has recently retired from the choral faculty at Indiana University, where he had a distinguished career in conducting and teaching. He contributed to the second edition of *Choral Conducting, A Symposium* by Decker and Herford, which was first published by Prentice-Hall in 1973.

Margaret Hillis

Margaret Hillis was a signature figure in the Chicago music scene, serving as conductor of the Civic Orchestra of Chicago and the Elgin Symphony Orchestra. She received nine Grammy awards for her work with the Chicago Symphony Chorus, America's first professional symphony chorus. She founded the group in 1957 and directed it until 1994. In 1957, she became the first woman to conduct the Chicago Symphony Orchestra. Her résumé also includes serving as an assistant to Robert Shaw and conducting engagements with numerous symphony orchestras across the United States.

Ann Howard Jones

Ann Howard Jones serves as Professor of Music and Director of Choral Activities at Boston University. Her association with Robert Shaw included her post as Assistant Conductor for Choruses for the Atlanta Symphony Orchestra and service as Musical Assistant with the Robert Shaw Chamber Singers and Festival Singers. She conducts the Boston University Tanglewood Institute Young Artists Choruses and maintains an extensive schedule of guest conducting throughout the country.

Helen Kemp

Professor Emeritus of Voice and Church Music at Westminster Choir College, Helen Kemp has trained children and teachers in the art of choral singing for more than six decades. A lyric soprano who developed a substantial career as an opera and oratorio performer, Kemp was drawn to the field of children's choir by her belief in young people's potential for artistic and personal growth. Kemp and her late husband, John, served as founding members of the Choristers Guild, the international organization for children's choirs.

Morten Lauridsen

Morten Lauridsen has served as Professor of Composition at the University of Southern California Thornton School of Music for more than 30 years. His works have earned a permanent place in the standard vocal repertoire of the twentieth century. While Lauridsen was Composer in Residence of the Los Angeles Master Chorale from 1994–2001, Maestro Paul Salamunovich and the Chorale recorded a Grammy-nominated CD of his compositions, *Lux Aeterna*.

Mary Lynn Lightfoot

Mary Lynn Lightfoot is one of today's foremost writers of choral music. Her music runs the gamut from warm and lush to rhythmic and energetic, and always displays careful attention to text, ranges, and accompaniments. The Choral Editor for Heritage Music Press, the educational division of The Lorenz Corporation, Lightfoot has authored numerous commissions and is in frequent demand as a guest conductor/clinician.

Donald S. Marsh

Early in his career Donald Marsh was involved in the theater, concert and TV world of New York City as an actor, choreographer and teacher. For three decades he served on the staff of the First Presbyterian Church of Port Jervis, New York, directing plays and musicals as well as conducting choirs. Marsh and his colleague, Richard K. Avery, have published more than 150 songs in songbooks and hymnals.

David McKechnie

David McKechnie is the retired pastor of Grace Presbyterian Church in Houston, Texas, and is currently serving as Interim Senior Pastor of the First Presbyterian Church of Houston.

Alice Parker

Alice Parker's life work has been in choral and vocal music, combining composing, conducting and teaching in a creative balance. Her arrangements with Robert Shaw of folksongs, hymns and spirituals form an enduring repertoire for choruses all around the world. She continues composing in many forms. In 1985, she founded Melodious Accord, Inc., a nonprofit group that presents choral concerts, sponsors workshops, symposia and her many professional appearances, and provides training for composers, conductors and song leaders.

Robert Shaw

The name Robert Shaw has been synonymous with choral music for several decades. His early recordings with the Robert Shaw Chorale, and those with the Robert Shaw Festival Singers and with the Atlanta Symphony Chorus and Orchestra defined the highest artistic achievement in both choral and choral/orchestral music. For several years, Mr. Shaw led a week-long workshop sponsored by Carnegie Hall where 160 auditioned singers came together to rehearse eight hours a day. A final Carnegie Hall concert, with orchestra, culminated the experience. When Arturo Toscanini saw Mr. Shaw work, he reportedly said, "I have found my choral maestro." Mr. Shaw has influenced several generations of choral conductors in this county and abroad.

Arturo Toscanini

Widely regarded as one of the greatest conductors of all time, Italian Arturo Toscanini came to the United States in 1937 to escape Fascist Italy. The NBC Symphony Orchestra was created for him, and soon both Toscanini and the orchestra became well known to the American public through radio broadcasts and tours. Another first for Toscanini was his extended appearances on live television, which began in the late '40s when Robert Shaw served as choral director for the choral/orchestral works.

Fred Waring

The career of Fred Waring featured longevity, vision and versatility. The career of "The Man Who Taught America How to Sing," spanned more than seven decades. A true pioneer, he contributed to the music industry via vaudeville, movies, radio, recordings, Broadway, television and the concert stage, bringing quality performances to the American public via broadcasts and extensive coast-to-coast tours. Recognized by both MENC and ACDA, Waring is also the recipient of the Congressional Gold Medal for achievements as composer/musical director/educator.

William Vennard

William Vennard's *Singing: The Mechanism and the Technic* has long been a resource for teachers of singing, researchers and singers themselves. Although the last edition was published in 1967, Vennard's influence has endured. A renowned vocal pedagogue, Vennard's most famous student was mezzo-soprano Marilyn Horne.

Notes

Introduction

1. Alice Parker, *Creative Hymn Singing,* 2nd ed. (Chapel Hill, NC: Hinshaw Music, Inc., 1976).

Chapter One

1. Joseph A. Musselman, *Dear People* (Bloomington: Indiana University Press, 1979), 174–175.

2. Alice Parker, *Melodious Accord Newsletter,* vol. 1 (Fall 2006): 3–4.

Chapter Two

1. Harold A. Decker and Julius Herford, *Choral Conducting: A Symposium,* 2nd ed. (Englewood Cliffs, NJ: Prentice-Hall, 1997).

2. James Jordan, *The Musician's Soul: A Journey Examining Spirituality for Performers, Teachers, Composers, Conductors, and Music Educators* (Chicago: GIA Publications, 1999).

3. Julius Herford, "The Conductor's Search," *Choral Journal* 38, no. 6 (December, 1991): 22–23.

4. Gordon Paine, "Score Selection, Study and Interpretation," in *Up Front! Becoming the Complete Choral Conductor,* ed. Guy Webb (Boston: ECS Publishing, 1993), 33.

5. Roger Fiske, "The Viennese Classical Period" in *Choral Music: A Symposium,* ed. Arthur Jacobs (London: Pelican Books, 1963), 170.

Chapter Three

1. James Jordan, *Evoking Sound: Fundamentals of Choral Conducting and Rehearsing* (Chicago: GIA Publications, 1996).

2. Dennis Keene, "An Interview with Margaret Hillis," *The American Organist* 26, no. 1 (January, 1992).

3. Ibid.

Chapter Four

1. Kenneth Jennings, *Sing Legato: A Collection of Original Studies in Vocal Production and Musicianship* (San Diego: Neil A. Kjos Music Co., 1982).

2. William Vennard, *Singing: The Mechanism and the Technic* (Ann Arbor, MI: Edwards Brothers, 1949).

Chapter Five

1. Roger Deschner, *Your Ministry of Singing in the Church Choir* (Nashville: Discipleship Resources, 1990), 13–14.

Chapter Six

1. Edna Clay, "Learning Styles," *Alabama Reprise,* 1997, no. 1: 1, 5.

2. Sally Herman, *In Search of Musical Excellence: Taking Advantage of Varied Learning Styles* (Dayton, OH: Roger Dean Publishing Co., 1994), 26–27.

3. David Keirsey and Marilyn Bates, *Please Understand Me: Character and Temperament Types* (Del Mar, CA: Prometheus Nemesis Books, 1984).

Chapter Seven

1. Alice Parker, "Remembering Robert Lawson Shaw," *Voice of Chorus America* 22, no. 4 (Summer 1999): 14–15.

Chapter Eight

1. Fred Pratt Green, *When in Our Music God Is Glorified* lyrics (Carol Stream, IL: Hope Publishing Co., 1972).

2. Sydney Carter, *Lord of the Dance,* arranged by John Ferguson (Boston: ECS Publishing, 1963).

3. Terry York and David Bolin, *The Voice of Our Congregation: Seeking and Celebrating God's Song for Us* (Nashville: Abingdon Press, 2005), 7–8.

4. Garth Bolinder, "Finding Your Worship Voice," *Leadership: A Practical Journal for Church Leadership* 15, no. 2 (Spring 1994): 26–33.

5. John Yarrington, *Somebody's Got My Hymnal: Another Lighthearted Look at Choir Directing* (Nashville: Abingdon Press, 2004), 63–64.

6. John L. Bell, *The Singing Thing: A Case for Congregational Singing* (Chicago: GIA Publications, 2000), 141–149.